What's *Still* Right with the Church of England

What's *Still* Right with the Church of England

The Revd Canon David Jennings

Rector, Burbage with Aston Flamville
Canon Theologian, Leicester Cathedral

Winchester, UK
Washington, USA

First published by Circle Books, 2013
Circle Books is an imprint of John Hunt Publishing Ltd., Laurel House, Station Approach,
Alresford, Hants, SO24 9JH, UK
office1@jhpbooks.net
www.johnhuntpublishing.com
www.circle-books.com

For distributor details and how to order please visit the 'Ordering' section on our website.

Text copyright: David Jennings 2012

ISBN: 978 1 78099 477 2

A CIP catalogue record for this book is available from the British Library.

Design: Stuart Davies

Printed and bound by CPI Group (UK) Ltd, Croydon, CR0 4YY

We operate a distinctive and ethical publishing philosophy in all
areas of our business, from our global network of authors to
production and worldwide distribution.

CONTENTS

Foreword

Canon David Jennings, as Rector of Burbage with Aston Flamville, Canon Theologian at Leicester Cathedral, and Diocesan Officer for Church and Society, is a senior priest within the Diocese of Leicester.

Canon Jennings is passionate about the Church of England and its continued mission within our nation. He strongly believes in the importance of the parochial system, for the Church to minister to all, regardless of Church attendance, class, ethnicity, gender, faith or sexual orientation. For Canon Jennings, the Church of England is an inclusive institution which is open and welcoming to everyone within the parish. This has been the Church's inherited tradition and such should not be discarded lightly or wantonly.

In this sense, the title of this book, referring back to one by a previous Bishop of Leicester, is both relevant and apposite for the Church of England's continued place in the life of our nation, its communities and its parishes. It is also a challenging book, which could be of great benefit to clergy and congregations who have concern about the positioning of the Church in society. Bishop Williams asked the question, 'what's right with the Church of England', but as an affirmation in 1966; David Jennings asks the further question in the affirmative, 'what's still right with the Church of England' in 2012 and beyond. It is interesting to note how many of the issues identified in 1966 are still 'live' issues for the Church some 46 years later.

Not everyone will agree with all of Canon Jennings' analyses or suggestions. However, all are worthy of examination and consideration. In particular, he emphasises the continued importance of the occasional offices of baptism, marriage and funerals for parishioners as a significant point of contact with those not directly involved with the life of the Church, and notes how many still look to their parish church to provide what are often called 'rites of passage'. The Church of England will ignore this continued demand and expectation at its peril, and would fail in its duty and responsibility to all within the parish. Canon Jennings' affirmation of liberalism may not engender universal support, but it is an important debate for the Church within the contemporary context. His discussion concerning the discipline of marketing as a tool for Church engagement reflects his own research about such in the diocese in 1996, and for which he was awarded an M.Phil from the University of Loughborough in 1998.

I would commend this book as part of an ongoing debate and discussion about the Church of England in 2012, and I welcome David Jennings' conviction, which is clearly evidenced in the book, that there really is something still right about the Church of England, even though there needs to be some critical evaluation as to how it continues to exercise ministry and challenge within our nation.

Rt Rev Tim Stevens
Bishop of Leicester
July, 2012

Preface

It is 2012 and I have been a priest in the Church of England for 37 years. Ministry has been varied: a curate in a large urban parish in the Black Country, director of a multi-faith agency and priest in Handsworth, Birmingham, vicar of a mining parish and bishop's chaplain for community relations, rector of a large suburban parish for the past 25 years, and Canon Theologian of Leicester Cathedral. Within this period, I have run a business, been a social worker, sat on a government quango, been a local councillor and worked with a variety of voluntary agencies. I write as a parish priest!

Whilst some of these experiences have been outside of parochial life and structures, my conviction remains that our parish churches and parish clergy are not only essential ingredients for the life of the Church and the proclamation of the Gospel, but also have much life yet to offer and to give to our communities and nation. This conviction exists in part through personal experience and observation, and perhaps contradicts the many attempts to seek fresh expressions of the Church, within the context of what is deemed as a mission-shaped Church and agenda. Some, however, would argue, and with justification, for what is termed a 'mixed economy' ecclesiology. Whilst these attempts and developments possess laudable intent, they function primarily from a belief that the Church is in a state of terminal decline and needs some life-saving resuscitation. Without doubt, there are many parts of the Church that give cause for concern in terms of viability, support and relevance. However, it is my belief that the factors behind such difficulties and concerns are internal to the Church, and reside primarily, although not exclusively, in a failure to engage sufficiently and practically with local communities through service and availability of buildings, people and ministers. In this respect, the

Church of England can reach those parts of communities which others may not. It is my experience that communities value their Church and clergy when such are engaged with the whole life of the community and the people who reside and sometimes work in our parishes. If the Church loves and cares for the people, they in turn may love and care for the Church.

Much research concerning the problems and issues facing the Church is undertaken within the Church and rarely with the wider population. Furthermore, one of the major indices of decline is that of Church attendance, which has always been subject to considerable variation over many centuries and for a variety of reasons. The real danger that the Church faces is the temptation to retreat and withdraw to the 'comfort zone' of increasing certainty and exclusivity that further withdraws from the issues and concerns of the vast majority of people who do not attend, or subscribe to perceived positions represented by a narrowing Church. In addition, many do not understand what a fresh expression Church may be like and might be concerned as to what a mission-shaped agenda may require. Such is apart from any linguistic or terminological confusions that are represented by these definitions.

I believe, therefore, that there is something still very right about the Church of England as such has been received and is experienced. Any talk of its demise is premature, to say the least. Some re-evaluation and mild resuscitation may be necessary in places. However, such should or need not entail 'throwing the baby out with the bathwater', but rather requires a positive assessment of the Church within communities, the parishes. The Church of England exists for and ministers to parishioners, and not solely to congregations.

David Jennings, July, 2012

Introduction

In order to assess some of the issues facing the Church of England today and possible and appropriate responses, it is the intention of this book to journey back 46 years with a critical evaluation of a book published in 1966 entitled 'What's Right with the Church of England' by Ronald Ralph Williams, then Bishop of Leicester (Lutterworth Press, 1966). The purpose, in part, is to indicate that many of the issues of 2012 were present in actual or embryonic form in the 1960s, but also to illustrate that what was considered right about the Church of England in 1966 might still be right for the Church today, although in a significantly changed environment. The task is, in part, analytical but also hermeneutical, in that some of the responses to the issues for the Church today would not have required the same responses as were considered and available 46 years ago. In this sense, this paper can be considered a sequel to Bishop Williams' paean, albeit one that faces the contemporary issues for the Church.

The purpose is not to engage in some form of ecclesiastical nostalgia, but rather to apply a methodology to the concerns of the Church that was not applicable in a past age in order to identify what can still be right for the Church of England in and throughout the twenty-first century. For some, the responses to the issues will be too radical and too dissonant with what is understood to be the Church, let alone the essentials of Christian belief. However, if the Church of England is still to be right, it cannot avoid or evade the pressing issues of this century, and if it is to be the Church for the whole nation, and not just that of a gathered collection of 'true believers' or congregations, then it needs to possess both the vision and the courage to evaluate and perhaps accommodate the necessary and required changes. At its best the Church is a living organism that resonates and engages with the things of God for his/her people within their various and varied situations and locations. Primary amongst the latter are the parishes of our nation, served by the parish priests of the Church.

It is the belief of the author that if the Church of England cannot or fails to address both the critical issues that exist both within the secular and ecclesiastical worlds, then its decline, not just in terms of supporters, but more significantly in value and appreciation, is a foregone conclusion. The Church cannot or should not exist in splendid isolation apart from the realities and issues that surround it. This has not been the history of the Church of England, and the temptation to be in exile should and needs to be resisted. The Church of England can be the Church for the people, of the people and by the people.

What's Right with the Church of England

Much evidence suggests that there is a deep-seated and widely-spread death-wish in the Church of England. On the other hand, this evidence can easily be given disproportionate weight, and should itself be analysed carefully to see to what exactly it is pointing. Some of it may be only a necessary facing of unpalatable facts, brought into promi-nence in the hope that thereby the Church should not die but live. Some of it may spring from a larger vision of the unfolding future, when even the best that has been would be subsumed into something infinitely richer than anything previously known(What's Right with the Church of England', R R Williams. Lutterworth Press, 1966)

The Rt Rev Dr Ronald Ralph Williams was Bishop of Leicester from 1953 to 1978. Prior to consecration, he was Principal of St John's Theological College in Durham. Although from an evangelical background, he was not constrained by such, but possessed a conservative disposition especially in matters of morals and ethics. It is clear from his book that he greatly valued the Church of England and its mission and ministry to the nation. This is especially true in respect of establishment, and the relationship of the Church with the state. It could be argued that such was not a difficult position to hold in 1966 when matters concerning the Church were very different to those of the early twenty-first century. Williams, however, was also somewhat of a visionary. He was able to identify issues for the Church that whilst not critical in 1966 became significant, if not problematic, over the ensuing 46 years. In this respect, Williams was able to read the signs of the times.

i) Parish Churches

In the first chapter of his book, entitled 'The Death-Wish', Williams focuses on a number of key issues. Amongst them was the need to maintain and care for ancient parish churches. Whilst acknowledging the increasing costs associated with our parish churches, Williams writes:

> *It would be wrong to deny that all these are real facts, and their combined force is considerable. But on the other side are weighty considerations, too hastily overlooked by the "levellers". To begin with, the Church finds itself, willy-nilly, the trustee not only of the greatest and most beautiful buildings in the country – our cathedrals – but also, in almost every village, of the most ancient, the most lovely, and the most loved building to be found there. Each of these is a shrine of endless personnel and corporate memories. The Church may get little praise for preserving them, but it will certainly get plenty of blame for letting them fall into ruin. Unfair, but true! The Church may often have to face unpopularity, but unpopularity arising from a breach of trust is not a very good starting point for evangelistic efforts!(ibid)*

ii) Occasional Offices

Williams identifies a number of other areas of concern within the life of the Church and which, for many, present significant challenges. These include what are called the occasional offices of baptism, marriages and funerals. He writes that for:

> *…..an increasing number of our clergy and theological students, the whole "folk-religion" aspect of the Church's life is anathema. "Holy things to the holy" is their motto, and the prospect of baptizing babies from homes of non-Christians, or non-practising Christians, is a heavy burden on their consciences. So also is it for them to marry those whose Church connections are so tenuous as to appear non-existent. So, finally, is it for them to bury, with prayers of Christian hope, those who have fallen far short of their standard of Christian faith and practice. (ibid)*

iii) Ecumenism

The question of Church of England identity is posed by both the development of the world-wide Anglican Communion, and the increasing ecclesial co-operation between different churches within a developing series of relationships as represented by the ecumenical movement. In some parts of the world, such as South India, there has been formal unity between former separated churches, with the distinct possibility of similar schemes in England. Issues concerning the nature of ministry, as represented in the Church of England by the orders of bishops, priests and deacons, and the liturgical focus provided by the 1662 Book of Common Prayer, together with variants, also raises issues of identity in terms of relationships with non-Episcopal and non-liturgical churches. Related to this is the issue of liturgical reform and change within the Church of England. Williams summarises the issues:

> *Parish ministries, teaching and doctrine, ancient buildings, occasional offices, ecumenical changes, liturgical reform, ministerial functions – all these are exposed to radical re-appraisal. Self-criticism is the order of the day. (ibid)*

However, he concludes:

> *Change is inevitable, as one of my fellow-bishops has said, but not all change is good. I believe that many in the Church will think twice before abandoning what has served many generations well, and may yet, purged and chastened by failure and criticism, lead England forward in the paths of service, unity, godliness and peace. (ibid)*

iv) Doctrine

In spite of having roots in the conservative (some would say, traditional) and evangelical stream of Church of England ecclesiology, Williams is not afraid to acknowledge areas of difficulty and tension within the Church, but also to consider what some would consider more radical developments. It is clear that in the Church of the mid-sixties and in more contemporary culture, there are differences of opinion concerning supposedly fundamental beliefs relating to interpretation of scripture and received Christian doctrine, for example in respect of the virgin birth of Jesus or his bodily resurrection. The creeds of the Christian faith are, for some if not many, problematic. Williams writes:

> *Then, at a more serious level, there have been new discussions about the obviously "supernatural" statements in the Creeds, especially those concerning the manner of Our Lord's Birth, and concerning the resurrection and Ascension ..... (I)t is not <u>absolutely</u> impossible to combine a radically sceptical view of the Gospel stories with a willingness to say the Creeds <u>ex animo</u>, though this requires a skill in mental gymnastics far beyond the comprehension of the ordinary man..... (T)here is, of course, nothing very new about this. The Doctrinal Commission of 1922-38 noted the existence of such views among responsible Churchmen, and did not condemn them out of hand. (ibid)*

As well as raising and articulating concerns about the creeds, Williams also notes the problem of the 39 Articles of Religion, and he acknowledges that the creeds refer primarily to the evolution and determination of the belief of the Church in the controversies of the first five centuries of the evolving Church's life. Williams' concerns pre-date by at least two decades views relating to Church doctrine as espoused by such as David Jenkins, Don Cupitt, Richard Holloway and Jack Spong, amongst others. He suggests that the briefer the creeds are, the better:

> *....for only when they are very brief can the vast mass of the would-be faithful get hold of their main assertions. Thus the brief summary*

of the Creeds given in the Catechism is about the best credal statement in the Prayer Book. It is a great pity that it is not more widely known. The question is asked, after recital of the Apostles' Creed, "What dost thou chiefly learn in these Articles of thy Belief?", to which the answer is given, "First, I learn to believe in God the Father, who hath made me and all the world. Secondly, in God the Son who hath redeemed me and all mankind. Thirdly, in God the Holy Ghost, who sanctifieth me and all the elect people of God". (ibid)

Although Williams is clearly identifying a problem with traditional and credal affirmations, the clauses advocated in the catechism are far removed from the former Bishop of Durham, Dr David Jenkins' much later re-writing as 'God is; he is as he is in Jesus, and there is hope'. Such perhaps was foreseen by Williams when he asserts:

The modern Christian is not expected to look on the Creeds as infallible, in the sense that no phrase in them could possibly be better expressed. It would be incredible if statements drawn up sixteen hundred years ago expressed perfectly the thoughts of those who live in a totally different world. (ibid)

v) Ethics

Williams has always been considered much more conservative when it comes to issues of ethics and morals. 'Whatever the bible teaches, then, about morals, the Church teaches', he asserts. Although affirming the Bible and the Prayer Book as primary sources for moral insight and requirement, it is again to the Catechism that Williams turns 'to sketch in the details of the moral demands of the Christian life'. He focuses particularly upon issues of sexual morality and writes:

No, the current criticism of traditional morality does not arise from any formal difficulty about the moral demands laid down in the Prayer Book. It arises almost entirely in one realm, the realm of personal relationships. (ibid)

Williams acknowledges the changed and changing circumstances of approaches to sexuality, especially amongst young people. However, he upholds what he considers to be traditional teaching that, whilst exercising love and compassion towards those who deviate from the Church's position concerning fidelity within marriage, it is the latter that must be upheld and maintained as the standard for sexual relationships.

vi) Worship

When it comes to the worship of the Church, Williams is able to acknowledge the traditional pattern of 8.00 am Holy Communion, then Matins at 11.00 am, afternoon Sunday School and Evensong, with which he was familiar as a boy. However, he recognises that such is a world unknown to a younger generation, and is able to say that '(m)ore satisfactory liturgical arrangements have come to the fore'. Williams clearly sees value in the development of the Parish Communion, often replacing the traditional format of 8.00 am Communion and 11.00 am Matins. He sees this development as opening up a full sacramental life for large numbers, and the possibility of the whole family attending Church together. The preparation of the Sunday lunch is still a consideration! Although Williams identifies a loss in the solemn and quiet reverence of the 8 o' clock and the great morning canticles in Matins, he can write, '(I)n spite of all this there is much to be thankful for'. However, he still sees a significant place for the continuation of Prayer Book Evensong, even though some criticisms can be made, and having to acknowledge 'the counter-attraction of many popular television programmes'.

Williams suggests that the value and strength of Church of England worship is not just to be found within the pages of the

Prayer Book, as important as such has been for the Church's liturgy and formation. Rather, it is to be experienced as both Catholic and Reformed, and within the context of local communities with 'the changing seasons of the Christian Year with all their accompaniments in liturgy, decorations and song', familiar and much loved hymns, the churches themselves, and particular times of celebration including baptism, Holy Matrimony and burial, all of which touch local communities beyond those within regular congregations. The Church of England offers regular public Sunday worship in its parishes, and fulfills the spiritual, if occasional, requirements of its parishioners.

vii) Ministry

In considering the ministry of the Church and the pastoral system, Williams is even more forthright in identifying changes in emphasis and practice. He notes that it was not many years previous when no-one within the Church of England would have questioned the episcopal system, the three-fold orders of bishops, priests and deacons, the territorial parish and the pastoral system. There were, of course, challenges to such from both the Free Churches and the Roman Catholic Church, although even in this respect there were changes and hope for possible convergence. Williams identifies issues such as the state appointment of bishops, their remoteness of style, life and dress and their lack of qualification as theological teachers as being problematic. He also suggests that the parish clergy are not much better. Their parishes are either too large or too small, they are chosen from too small a sector of the population, often too many are from Oxbridge colleges, they lack experience in business or industry and they frustrate the laity. Williams also identifies the ambiguity of the role and purpose of deacons.

Whilst acknowledging that the three-tier structure of Anglican ministry cannot be read simply as a continuity from New Testament or even patristic times, nevertheless 'every grouping of Christian people has in practice some hierarchy' and '(d)oubtless every one of these systems could be supported by isolated texts or passages from the Bible, or by Patristic precedents'. Williams' view is that the three-fold ministry, as well as providing an organic link with the Church of past ages, works well. He also believes that episcopacy will be built into Church unity schemes and that '(I)t is an odd moment for the Church of England to get half-hearted and cynical about its own episcopate'.

The order of priests or presbyters can have a variety of meanings and understandings, which can include pastor and teacher as well as a more sacerdotal emphasis. Williams affirms the whole Church to be priestly, but that the individual priest acts as the 'spokesman and mouthpiece of the Church'. He continues:

> ....it is clear that in the Anglican system the Church is gathered into local units, sufficiently coherent to live and worship together, and that the "cure and government of the souls of the "parishioners" are committed to men who belong to this second order of "priesthood". To them is delegated by the bishop the right to baptize (apart from emergencies in which anyone may do so), the right to celebrate the Eucharist. The right to preach and to admonish, to visit the sick and whole, and to do what is needed in the services of Holy Matrimony and Burial of the Dead. To the bishop is reserved the right of Institution, Confirmation and Ordination. (ibid)

Williams continues to recognise that the Anglican way of handling deacons is one of the Church's weaker spots. He says very little more.

Following consideration of the ministry of the Church, Williams then examines the pastoral system, giving what he describes as 'a brief sketch of the pastoral system of the Church as I have known it and tried to work it', whilst not shutting his eyes to failures and limitations. He writes:

Whether the diocese or the parish is the essential unit of Church life is disputable. For practical purposes the ordinary layman comes up against the Church in its parochial setting, and the independence and responsibility of the parish priest is a very precious part of our heritage. (ibid)

Williams, as one might expect of a bishop, emphasises the importance and significance of the episcopacy, and his cathedral church as a focus of unity and the diocese. He sees much value in the rite of confirmation as an episcopal rite but acknowledges the fact that many baptised as infants do not appear as confirmees in teenage years. This, of course, is a continuing phenomenon, as also is the increase in adult confirmations which Williams identifies. However, in spite of an episcopal emphasis, Williams still affirms the ministry of parish priests and illuminates the difficulties of parochial ministry. He writes:

…..I do not want in any way to underrate the vital importance of the work of the parish priest. It ought to be more widely known that perhaps the bishop's biggest single task, in terms of hours of work, consists in nothing else than the maintenance in quantity and quality of the parish clergy. (ibid)

He continues to assert that many of the questions of ministry arise at the parochial level. Five points of concern are identified which include the relevance of the priest in modern society: the need for more collaborative work with the laity, the loneliness of much ministry especially in rural areas, the attempt to discharge an 'all purpose ministry' in an age of specialisation, and the priest being called upon to exercise 'religious rites for all and sundry', including those with no real interest in the Church. He then goes on to point out the decline in the numbers ordinands, that candidates 'drop out', and that curates desire any work than that of a parish priest, seeking chaplaincy work as an alternative.

There are some responses, if not solutions to the problems and issues Williams identifies. Difficulties, he admits, are not always perceptible to a visiting bishop. He has some guidance to offer:

The parson must, for example, be able to make Church life inter-esting. He must have sufficient imagination and initiative to put before his people projects that they will think worthwhile, and for which they will work together. He must be reliable – if he says he will visit X, he must do so, and promptly. He must be friendly, outgoing, cheerful, and have a quick, intuitive sympathy, especially with those in trouble. He must be able to bring to his people a dimension of life without which their lives would be impoverished. For this he must have his own inner resources of prayer, faith and love. Given these qualities, the work of the English parish priest still frequently succeeds in the building up and maintaining "a live parish", a living centre of worship, witness fellowship and service. We cannot ask for more. (ibid)

Williams acknowledges different types of parishes which require differing ministerial emphases. Whilst the parish priest in the country farms and the villages can still exercise a prominent and focused ministry, in the new housing developments such is not so easy. He suggests that in such areas 'the Church of England cannot, and should not, in all cases hope to provide it alone.' Williams asserts that suburban ministry is easier, but points out that there is a real problem with city centre churches where parochial residents have been replaced with shops, offices and factories which are empty at weekends.

viii) Establishment

Williams then considers that particular Church of England conundrum, the relationship with the state or establishment. He gives a brief survey of the first 50 years of the twentieth century and various reforms in Church governance. Mention is made of the conflict between the Church and parliament over Prayer Book reform in the late 1920s. Williams acknowledges a frustration amongst many clergy with establishment, including that of senior ecclesiastical appointments. However, by the 1960s a number of changes had been effected, especially in respect of liturgical matters. There are inevitable problems with appointments when church unity schemes are considered. Particular schemes including Methodists and Presbyterians have encountered difficulty not just with the possible incorporation of episcopacy but more particularly in respect of the manner of appointments.

In seeking to address the issue from the Church of England perspective, Williams points out that all churches have some relationship with the state, whether that be of persecution as in communist regimes, or of complete separation as in France and America. 'In England we have a State Church, with many duties and some privileges arising from that connection'. He continues that '(f)or all practical purposes "Establishment" as a feature of the Church of England means "special recognition".' Williams spells this out as meaning the sovereign is crowned within an Anglican Communion service by the Archbishop of Canterbury, a number of bishops have seats in the House of Lords (which has always been the case except in the Commonwealth period), and bishops and deans (and a number of canons and incumbents) are appointed by the Crown. He sees no problem in this process when he writes:

> The Church must remember that appointment by the Crown is not entirely to the disadvantage of the Church. Quite apart from the question of whether the Crown's processes do or do not produce the best men (and a bishop is poorly placed either to make or deny that assertion) the fact that the bishops are appointed by the Crown indicates that religion and the Church are matters of importance to the State itself. Much as this system is disliked and criticised in

modern times, I strongly suspect that a bishop who is nominated by the Crown to a certain see has an acceptance and an authority from the start different in nature from that which would be his if his election arose only from some process in the inner circle of the Church itself. (ibid)

Williams, however, then moves on to consider what he terms 'Establishment at the grass roots!' This is the offering of baptism, marriage and burial for all within the parish. He quotes a priest who, after a year in America, regretting the gathered congregation ecclesiology and the delight 'to come back here and to be the "person" of a parish as well'. Williams criticises those in favour of disestablishment who assume 'there is one hard and fast line which distinguishes members of the Church from non-members'. There is, of course, a line between the baptised and the unbaptised, the confirmed and the non-confirmed, the regular communicant and the irregular communicant but he warns:

.......the idea of a very shadowy line between Church members and non-members is anathema to those who wish to treat England exactly as if it was a "mission field" in the overseas sense of that phrase. But before they draw hasty conclusions about what should be done, they should take note that the "sect approach", the setting aside of certain persons and groups on the basis of a strict membership test, has been tried and tried again in the history of the Church, including the history of Christianity in England. Many of these sects have just disappeared. Others are waning fast. Some have prospered. (ibid)

Williams believes that to offer Baptism to all children may be much closer to the basic idea of the Gospel than to impose tests:

Baptism, even indiscriminate Baptism, would express the unconditional love and mercy of God for all far better than Baptism admin-

istered on the strength of some righteous performance, either on the part of the candidate or his family …..but the whole modern idea that Baptism is to be looked on as a reward for pious practice, and not as an undeserved gracious favour given by God, is in my view to be deplored. (ibid)

Whilst Williams holds the link between Church, Crown and parliament in high regard, seeing such as indicative and representative of the role of religion, and the Christian religion in particular, within society, nevertheless he affirms the practical outworking of establishment within the context of parochial ministry. He feels that establishment is under threat from within the Church.

Williams writes positively and enthusiastically about issues of Church unity. He is clearly hopeful, but also realistic of difficulties and obstacles. In the first instance he deals with the split between Rome and the Eastern Orthodox Church in 1054, and current signs of rapprochement. He also identifies signs of hope and new relationships between Rome and the leading Protestant Churches. Williams observes the many changes within the Roman Catholic Church that make moves towards unity more possible than would have been the case only a few years previous. This is particularly the case in respect of liturgical changes. There are other significant ecumenical endeavours and unity schemes and realities in other parts of the world.

Williams addresses the ecumenical scene in England especially with regard to union with Methodists and Presbyterians, although such does not exclude other denominations. There are, of course, different theological and ecclesiological emphases, but architecturally an Anglican Church looks quite different from a Free Church chapel, but, as he writes:

Then the Church of England has bishops, and in practice this means much more than the fact that some of her ministers are differently named and differently garbed from others. It implies that the ministry of the Church "comes from above", not from below. Whilst the lay voice is heard at Ordination in the Church of England ……in the Free Churches the ministers are either "called" by the local church, or appointed by some synodical conference…..There are rather more services "taken out of a book" in the Church of England, and the Holy Communion is given a prominence quite its own as compared with other services. (ibid)

Williams proceeds to ask the question what part the Church of England can play towards the unity of the Church. He is highly critical of Churches coming together to form a new Church arising both from the death of two or more denominations and preserving and enhancing the best that is in each. Is it not possible that in some sense they both become Churches and that they will remain a denomination when united? Williams looks back to the time when there was only the Church of England and that then the Church of England, by definition, was not a denomination. He affirms that all are members of the church by virtue of baptism 'even if they were for the time gathered in special societies as Baptists or Methodists'. Williams sees the Church of England as the framework round which 'the coming great Church' could grow and develop. There would be a concordat between Churches, ministers receiving episcopal ordination, local acts of union: '(t)he purpose would quite frankly be the building of a united Church round the fabric of the existing Church of England'. Williams observes the primacy of the Presbyterian Church of Scotland, the Roman Catholic Church in Ireland and one or more of the non-conformist Churches in Wales. However, episcopacy is the *sine qua non* of his proposals. For Williams, the Church of England is the historic Church, witnessing to continuity over many centuries. He raises the question:

.......whether the Church of England, which has so much to offer in the way of continuity, can find sufficient flexibility and adaptability to make it "a chariot of the gospel" in this age, which is so different from all those which have preceded it.'(ibid)

ix) Signs

Williams proceeds to identify and briefly comment on seven hopeful signs:

i)   The service of the family. He sees the Parish Communion being at the forefront of enabling families to worship together. Family ceremonies such as baptism, marriage and burial are still important and significant for many. The popularity of Mothering Sunday and Carol Services are a further indication of Church engagement. He writes:
Whatever other ministries may prove necessary, people will still live in homes and in families, and it is there that the Church must be ready to give them a service that is efficient, expert, relevant and understanding. (ibid)

ii)   The Emergence of Planned Giving. Whilst Williams was writing at a time when the historic endowments of the Church of England funded two-thirds of clergy stipends, parishes had to fund running costs, Church repairs and restoration. Williams could see that there was going to be an increased demand upon congregations and he was encouraged by the emergence of planned giving

iii) The 'conversion' of adults. Williams does not recognise the need for conversion in England in the same way that such would apply in a non-Christian country. His view is based upon increased numbers of adult baptism and confirmation candidates and he acknowledges various reasons for this. Such also applies to mature ordinands.

iv) New ideas in liturgy and architecture. Williams observes new Churches in new housing areas and significant re-ordering of Church interiors, especially in respect of nave altars. New liturgical services, including those associated with Lent, Holy Week and Easter, are signs of renewal. 'If many new ideas for Church services spring from a vitality of spirit (and they often have in the past), the Church of England may take hope – on this test it would seem to win rather high marks!'

v) The 'arrival' of the laity. Williams speaks mainly about Church governance, although lay involvement in the life of the Church includes the spiritual and doctrinal life. Writing in 1966, he sees hope in a new system of synodical government 'when the *whole* Church, bishops, priests, deacons and laity, will together carry the ultimate authority (under the Crown, if the "Royal Supremacy" remains) for the whole life of the Church'.

vi) The retreat and conference movement. Williams observes an increase in retreats and weekend conferences. Almost every diocese has a Retreat and Conference House. 'Few things have done more in our time to re-vitalize both clergy and laity than these new opportunities to explore together, free from distraction, in a holy and loving atmosphere, "what the Spirit says to the Churches".'

A new sense of mission. He makes a plea for keeping matters in proportion acknowledging the pre-eminent place for worship. However, worship becomes more real if the needs of others are 'vividly present in the minds of the worshipping fellowship' Williams affirms the role of various ministries in reaching out to others where they are. However, he does not suggest that these specialized ministries can ever be a substitute for residential ministries. Our society may be mobile, but, he asserts, most families still sleep somewhere or other, and that is the place where the Church must most obviously be ready to serve and help them in whatever ways are possible.

Williams is not unaware of the danger signals which may require a need to re-think the Church's work with perhaps a renewed evangelistic requirement. He does not think the Church is at this point yet! However, he expresses concern about the decline in vocations 'among men of normal age and good education' and continues:

> There will never be a revival of vocations unless young men see their parish priests fulfilling a real and essential role in society as they themselves understand it, and also see that society values this role. That is the real importance of the clergy being properly paid. It is not that we cannot or dare not ask for sacrifice. It is that if the community does not think a clergyman's work is worth equal pay with that of the teacher, the skilled technician, or, dare we say, the doctor, it is very hard for the teenage boy, looking at the world for the first time, to believe that it _is_ of equal value. (ibid)

Williams also expresses concern about theological and spiritual understanding amongst Church people: '(t)housands bought _Honest to God_, but how many read and understood it?' There is also the problem of too large an organisational structure for those who are called upon to support it. City Churches are cited as an example.

Williams concludes his book by raising the question of grounds for confidence. He observes the decline and fall of Churches throughout history, including that of error and even disappearance. Survival cannot be guaranteed. However, he suggests that it is possible to believe (and this can only be a matter of faith) that if a Church is faithful to its given task, God will continue to use and bless it. He concludes:

The Church of England may err, like any other Church. The Church of England may fail, like any other Church. But if it errs, and if it fails, it will not, in my view, do so because of any serious fault in its structure, its traditions and its belief, but only because its members have ceased to believe in God, to love and serve the Lord Jesus Christ, to live and worship together in the fellowship of the Holy Spirit, the Lord and giver of life. (ibid)

x) Conclusion

There can be little doubt as to Bishop Williams' love and confidence in the Church of England as he lived and experienced it in the mid 1960s. It is also somewhat ironic that some of the issues and even difficulties that confronted the Church in those days are still live issues some 46 years later, and the call for a response has echoes in the contemporary ecclesiastical scene. Some will have difficulty with the bishop's emphasis on personal morality, especially in respect of sexual engagement and marriage. Others will want to see a continuum of concern to issues of same-sex relationships and the affirmation of celibacy. Williams says nothing about the possibility of the ordination of women and his book reflects and refers entirely to male ministers. Fewer perhaps would want to assert the primacy and even pivotal role for the Church of England in matters of ecumenical relations and possible Church unity schemes, although some see the 'via media' of Anglicanism as possessing the possibility of drawing different and differing ecclesiologies together. It would be naïve to suggest that such would be easy let alone acceptable!

Williams, however, sees considerable merit in the established position of the Church of England. This has two dimensions: there are the formal arrangements that exist in respect of the Crown, and there is the pastoral and parochial responsibility that enables and effects an ecclesiological and ministerial engagement beyond the local congregation, and thereby to the parish as a whole. Williams values and affirms both dimensions. Whilst there is considerable contemporary concern about the former, especially in respect of senior ecclesiastical appointments and the right of Parliament to legislate for the Church, there is significant merit in understanding and experiencing the Church of England as a Church for all, and in particular for those who do not attend. The Elizabethan settlement of the sixteenth century, although now considerably dated, bequeathed a broad based and non-sectarian ecclesiology that reflects a theological impetus and identification with the incarnational principle of being and existing for all rather than just the few.

What, therefore, can Williams say to the Church of the emerging twenty-first century from the position of the very different but nevertheless rapidly changing context of the Church in the mid-1960s? There have been many changes over the ensuing 46 years, both in society and within the church. There can be little doubt that many of the certainties of British society in the immediate post-war years came under intense scrutiny and challenge in the 1960s. It is difficult to assess how much the Church as an institution, and the ordained ministry fully understood let alone experienced the rapidity of the changes of values, social, political and moral, that were occurring.

Dominic Sandbrook writes:

Although the sixties are often seen as a secular, even post-religious, age, in few decades of the twentieth century were religious issues so hotly and enthusiastically debated. ('White Heat: a History of Britain in the Swinging Sixties', Dominic Sandbrook. Little, Brown: London, 2006)

However, he goes on to note:

Indeed, there does seem to have been a sense in the early sixties that the foundations of British Christianity were finally crumbling under the harsh lights of modernity. (ibid)

A changing youth culture and the rejection of deference and authority inevitably posed an issue for the Church, which in many respects had relied upon a more structured and ordered society than that which was emerging. The deeply rooted establishment view of Church and State as twin pillars within an ordered society was questioned and questionable, both from within and without traditional ecclesiastical circles. It is clear that Williams, even as a very much establishment and conservative bishop, was not unaware of these challenges and was not afraid to address the same. The question is whether Williams was right in his assumption that there was something significantly and profoundly right about the Church of England even within the rapidly changing world of the mid 1960s, and, furthermore, whether there is still something right and of value about the Church of England as received and changing within the early years of the twenty-first century? This book seeks to address this fundamental question and to raise issues of concern for the continued existence of the Church of England. Can the Church face the issues that both confront its very existence and threaten its credibility? Are the Parish Church and parish priest able to live, represent and present a Gospel, literally the 'good news', that truly reflects the life and spirit of Christ in a way that is both relevant and challenging to the age that is 46 years on from when Bishop Williams wrote his affirmation of the role, purpose and function of the Church of England?

Issues

Throughout the land there is a crisis of faith. Never mind the statistics, just go to any garden centre on a Sunday and you will see it. The Sabbath is reserved for picking out shrubs or maybe a trip to Do It All. Church pews are empty while car boot sales attract rows of bargain hunters. Jesus has not only to contend with the devilish pastime of DIY but also has rigorous competition from the telly and the bulk of the Sunday newspapers. And I haven't even got round to mentioning the truly godless among us who get all the spiritual replenishment we need by staying in bed. Sure, we go to Church for weddings, the odd christening, but on a Sunday morning? You've got to be joking. ('Ad Gloriam', Suzanne Moore in 'Guardian Weekend', 10th April, 1993)

There can be little doubt about the numerical decline of people attending Church which, with the exception of notable and prominent examples, has occurred over the past 40 years. Furthermore, few people can be unaware of financial pressures facing the Church, caused in part by declining numbers but, more significantly, by increasing costs and pension responsibilities. There are self-induced, but publicly represented internal tensions within the life of the Church, which further erode societal credibility in respect of the Church's relevance, and contributes towards increased marginalisation, if not alienation. It is the intention of this chapter to examine a number of contemporary issues facing the Church today with a view to identifying positive responses, if not signs of hope. The selection of issues is somewhat arbitrary, and there could be many others of equal significance and importance.

Perception and Position

From a visual perspective a Parish Church is often easily identified with a prominent spire or tower. Of course, such is not always the case, but the majority of Churches still possess a readily and easily identifiable location. Many people in a community, even with no connection to or knowledge of the local Parish Church, will still be able to direct enquiring strangers to the building. There would be a large number of business and retail outlets that would pay considerable sums for such a market position. The Church, therefore, should be very cautious about discarding such a valuable asset. A prominent and identifiable Church building still resonates with local communities and still has value. Martyn Percy writes:

> ....the (somewhat dubious) distinction between mission and mainte-
> nance is often a false dichotomy in the majority of parochial
> contexts, where the historic religious resonance of the church
> building will have a widespread (if sometimes unclear) spiritual
> significance. Thus, good maintenance of a building ('sermons in
> stone') is likely to be, de facto, good mission in any parochial context
> ('Shaping the Church: The Promise of Implicit Theology', Martyn
> Percy. Ashgate, 2010)

Williams writes positively about Church buildings, and in particular notes their historic connections with parishes and communities. A threatened Church building often engenders considerable support and resistance to possible closure. There is the attendant risk that a Church which closes says very clearly that the Church is either in terminal decline or, worse, has no vested or strategic interest in a particular parish. Whilst there may be cheaper buildings to utilise as a Church, a cost benefit analysis of the prominent and often historic building may suggest that it is better kept and perhaps more widely used.

There is another perception and positioning of the church within a community that is not just represented by the existence of a visible building. This is to do with how a community views the presence and existence of its Church, and the Church's ministers. A Church that is perceived and experienced as being concerned about its community, and existing to serve the same through positive and direct engagement, will score high in terms of added value as compared with an ecclesial community that exists purely and solely to serve, protect and increase its 'members'. The German theologian, Jurgen Moltmann once wrote, within the context of the relationship between the

Christian faith and other world religions, and which has relevance and implications beyond this particular issue:

> It (mission) thinks in terms of quantity and evolves strategies for "Church growth" ......But mission has another goal as well. It lies in the qualitative alteration of Life's atmosphere – of trust, feelings, thinking and acting. We might call this missionary aim to "infect" people, whatever their religion, with the spirit of hope, love and responsibility for the world. Up to now this qualitative mission has taken place by the way and unconsciously, as it were, in the wake of the "quantitative" mission. In the new world situation in which all religions find themselves, and the new situation of Christianity in particular, the qualitative mission directed towards an alteration of the whole atmosphere of life should be pursued consciously and responsibly. ('Christianity and the World Religions', Jurgen Moltmann, in 'Christianity and Other Religions' edited John Hick and Brian Hebblethwaite. Fount, 1980)

When a Church seeks the improvement of the quality of life for all, both in local terms of service to the community and that of wider global, social, environmental and political issues, it then exposes itself to the risk of relevance. Its position within society will be perceived as having both purpose and value. There is the consequential risk of support, though not necessarily in terms of increased congregations. A Church that is respected and valued within its community and beyond will be able with greater ease than otherwise to raise resources for programmes, buildings and mission.

It would be true to say that in many places parish priests and Church communities are engaged with and supportive of community activities, not least through involvement in local voluntary agencies, and thereby receive mutual support and respect. On the other hand, there would appear to be an increasing trend towards isolation and positive dis-engagement with what is often perceived and described as 'secular society'. Such can sometimes take on a combative if not 'jihadist' perspective, as Church people see themselves at odds with contemporary cultural values and practices. The mantle of being 'counter cultural' more often than not is located in attitudes and responses to issues of human sexuality and individual personal morality. There are some profound confusions and ambivalences in this ghetto-like ecclesiology as such engages or otherwise with the surrounding community and the rest of society.

In the late 1950s and early 1960s English society had a significant racist dimension. The reception given to first generation immigrants from the West Indies was that of overt discrimination both individual and institutional. Churches were no less unwelcoming to fellow Christians, the majority of whom were Anglican:

> Biggest shock was, one, the cold, and two, having gone to church for the very first time – so elated, so delighted that I'm coming from an Anglican church back home, I went to join in worship, and so I did – but after the service I was greeted by the vicar, who politely and nicely told me: "Thank you for coming. But I would be delighted if you didn't come back." And I said, "Why?" He said, "My congregation is uncomfortable in the company of black people." That was my biggest shock. I was the only black person in that congregation that Sunday morning, and my disappointment, my despair went with me and I didn't say anything to anyone about it for several months after that. (Carmel Jones, a future Pentecostal minister arriving in Britain, 1955, quoted in 'Family Britain', David Kynaston. Bloomsbury Publishing, 2009)

In this respect, the Churches mirrored the views and values of secular society and saw no contradiction let alone Gospel dissonance in such a position. However, by the middle to late 1970s, the Churches were in the forefront of condemning racism in wider society and Church leaders were prominent in anti-racist movements and were to be seen on anti-racist platforms. The founding of the ecumenical movement, Christians Against Racism and Fascism in 1978 represented a widespread Church movement in response to the recent electoral successes of the far-right National Front. There was significant credibility in this position, although by this time the government had passed the first Race Relations Act of 1976 making it a criminal offence to incite racial hatred and outlawing much discrimination. Other movements evidencing Church support included those of nuclear disarmament, housing, and liberal legislation such as that concerning homosexuality and abortion, although by no means was there universal ecclesiastical support for reform and change. However, it was in respect of the latter that many within the Church in the late twentieth and early twenty-first centuries have united to adopt not only a distinctively counter cultural position, but one that appears to many outside of the Church to be both illiberal and discriminating in a society which has progressed considerably in these matters. Whilst there can be justification for the Church proclaiming a counter cultural message in respect of certain issues, those concerning homosex-uality and woman's right to choose (subject to certain restrictions and limitations) are ones that can be criticised theologically, socially and politically. The result is increasing alienation and marginalization in respect of the perception and position of the Church in society.

A further area that encourages and entices many churches into introspection and insularity is the supposed and perceived challenge from what is termed militant atheism, as represented by, for example, the likes of Richard Dawkins (former Charles Simonyi Professor for the Public Understanding of Science at Oxford University and fellow of New College, Oxford), Peter Atkins and A C Grayling, who not only feel that God is a delusion, but also that religion is harmful. The reaction of many within the churches is disproportionately aggressive, even in the face of Dawkins' anti-religious polemic. Dawkins begins his best-selling book 'The God Delusion' (Bantam Press, 2006) with a quotation from Albert Einstein:

> *I don't try to imagine a personal God; it suffices to stand in awe at the structure of the world, insofar as it allows our inadequate senses to appreciate it.*

The quotation opens the first chapter of the book entitled 'A deeply religious non-believer'. Clearly, Dawkins and other fellow travellers present a significant challenge to religious belief and faith from what he and others would describe as a rigourist scientific perspective and methodology. There are many within the Church who dismiss this atheist scientist with a vigour that is often inconsistent or at odds not only with basic human respect, but also in such a manner that is profoundly opposite to the pursuit of open and free enquiry. Dawkins himself is not adverse to the expression of forthright opinion. The problem, however, with Dawkins for the Church is that much of his criticism of religion is unnervingly accurate, and his denial of God poses a valid challenge for those who rarely confront his/her existence, let alone face the inconsistencies of God's attributes and supposed actions, or inaction, within the world. Dawkins has consistently asserted the irrationality of belief in God and the grievous harm such has inflicted upon human society. He notes that while Europe is becoming increasingly secularised, the rise of religious fundamentalism, whether in the Middle East or Middle America, is dramatically and dangerously dividing opinion around the world. Furthermore, in many countries religious dogma from medieval times still serves to abuse basic human rights such as those of women and gay people. The difficulty for those concerned about the perception of the Church, and for the thinking and analytical Christian is that much of what

Dawkins attacks is valid, although it is far from the whole story. He sets up a recognisable caricature of religious belief and practices and then proceeds very effectively to demolish the same. It has to be acknowledged, however, that in many instances the caricature is accurate. There are many believers and many forms of religious practice and expression that leave much to be desired, and are worthy of criticism. Furthermore, in the eyes of many detractors, no one religion is better or worse than another. Also, many of the concepts and descriptions of God do not survive critical scrutiny. Those who possess a sense and experience of God need to accept the criticism, and work to find new and fresh ways of talking about God which makes sense to twenty-first century scientific knowledge, experience and discourse. It simply is no good relying on the old texts and the old language. The perception and position of the Church will largely be determined by its response to the challenges of contemporary scientific thought and philosophy, whether such be articulated by the likes of Richard Dawkins, or many others who may not be quite so hostile to the Church and religious faith and belief. Bishop Williams did not have to contend with militant atheism so widely held and expressed, but he was not unaware of the challenge and the need for the Church to be able to offer appropriate responses.

In summary, the position and perception of the Church is determined by a number of criteria. However, foremost amongst such are the location, visibility and value of the Church building, the engagement with and support for the local community by the Church, which would include credibility in respect of political, social and global issues and which impact upon people's lives, together with intelligent responses to scientific, philosophical and atheistic challenges to belief and religious practice. In many places and instances, the Church of England is able to respond positively to these issues and does so admirably. However, such is not universally the case.

ii) Resources and Finance

(t)hose who sustain the Church by their giving and voluntary service and those who have dedicated their lives to parish ministry have a right to expect some coherence in the way in which the resources they have provided are spent and the Church's ministry is deployed within their parishes. The proportion which lay people are now paying towards the cost of ministry is rising year by year and with this change has come an increased demand for greater account-ability for the way in which the Church's resources are used. The people of the church who are supporting it with their giving are rightly seeking a Church which is accountable and can demonstrate direction and vision. ('Working as One Body, 1995: the Report of the Archbishops' Commission on the Organisation of the Church of England.' Church House Publishing: London)

The issue facing the Church of England, and as identified by the Archbishops' Report, is the raising of sufficient resources to pay for the clergy, the maintenance of costly ancient buildings, and the funding of Church programmes and activities. However, because for many years considerable resources were devolved from the Church Commissioners, a body holding and adminis-tering significant historic national resources for the Church of England, to dioceses in order, primarily, to support the payment of the clergy, the Church of England, unlike many other denomi-nations, was shielded from the reality and necessity to pay for the clergy. For this reason, the Church was able to maintain a parochial ministry in many areas which it could not sustain if required from local resources. In recent years, the level of funding from the Church Commissioners has declined dramati-cally as it funds increasing amounts for pensions for retired clergy and widows, significant speculative losses in the property market in the late 1980s, and the costs of cathedral and episcopal ministry. This has simply meant that more money needs to be raised by the dioceses, which means, in effect, from the parishes, to pay for current clergy in post. Although the recently formed Church of England Pensions Board has assumed responsibility for pensions, the pressure has increased with the legislative requirement to ensure adequate funds for pensions and thereby to seek additional parochial funds for clergy pensions. The burden has fallen to the laity for the first time in the history of the Church of England to pay for their clergy, both in employment and in retirement. Inevitably, this has implications, for good or ill, on the relationship between clergy and laity, with both viewing such in terms of accountability. No longer can the parish priest, even with the legal protection tenure afforded by the freehold or common tenure, ignore the wishes, hopes, aspirations, needs and even demands of his/her parishioners.

The issue of resources and finances for the Church of England, given the aforementioned changes, focuses the reality of resource transfers from richer to poorer parishes. Such is necessary if the Church is truly to be national and have an effective and real presence in all areas and parts of society. There are inevitable tensions within such a reality which draws attention to affordability and viability. Permanent and unquestioned subsidy provokes changes concerning effectiveness. Robin Gill argues that:

> ...positive use of subsidy on a fixed term basis should replace the use of long-term subsidy to maintain existing structures. It is sometimes suggested that such concepts introduce secular management practices into churches. On the contrary, it cannot be stressed sufficiently that national churches already have (and have to have) a set of management practices. Unfortunately, those most widely used in Britain are increasingly recognised in other caring and educational bodies to be among the least effective available. ('The Myth of the Empty Church', Robin Gill. SPCK: London, 1993)

It is at this point that the issue of the financial viability, sustainability and continuity of the Church of England is most sharply focused. Williams was not unaware of this potential threat to the universal ministry and presence of the Church of England, and he acknowledged the efforts and commitments of many to secure additional parochial resources. What he was unable to perceive or foretell was the real depth of the emerging problem, and the challenge such would pose to the Church. Michael Hinton, writing some 30 years later than Williams, identifies the ecclesiological problem:

> *Never fully the Church of the nation, she is losing the claim to be the Church which serves the nation. She baptises fewer children, confirms fewer people, marries fewer adults, conducts smaller proportion of funerals. Lack of resources makes the pastoral ideals which have been her greatest strength less attainable. Her contributions to education and to social service though not insignificant, are increasingly marginal. Her political influence is waning. There are those who seek her disestablishment; should it take place, her place in national life would become even more peripheral than it is now. Above all, the parochial system, which is of the essence of historic Anglicanism, is collapsing under the strains imposed upon it by declining human and financial resources. ('The Anglican Parochial Clergy: a Celebration', Michael Hinton. London: SCM Press, 1994)*

There can be little doubt that the Church of England, in comparison with other churches, is well endowed and possesses considerable financial resources. However, it has costs that far exceed those of the other churches, and which draw upon the reality of being the Established Church for the whole nation, possessing significant numbers of clergy and related costs throughout the nation, and being responsible for the majority of the historic buildings of the nation. A diminution or elimination of any one of these would jeopardize the essential nature of the

Church of England and its distinctive, but still much-valued ministry. However, the threats are real.

What are the options in favour of securing the necessary resources and finance for the Church? Clearly, in the first instance there needs to be an adequate and robust examination of the use and deployment of existing resources, whether in the form of historic endowments or current voluntary giving. There should be a bias towards resource direction to the point of delivery of the prime focus of the Church's activity, namely the parishes, together with a critique of central costs, many of which would be easily and readily justifiable. Within this process and attitudinal disposition should be the recognition that the increasing proportion of the Church's income is coming from the voluntary giving of the person in the pew, and for whom the continuation of parochial ministry is of supreme importance.

At the same time, there is the need to increase and maximise income to the Church. It is often the case that such is best effected locally, as the reality and experience of the Church is tangibilised. The central Church structures and organisation are intangible and thereby difficult to market. Theodore Levitt posed the distinction between the tangible and intangible product as follows:

> The most important thing to know about intangible products is that the customer usually doesn't know what he's getting until he doesn't. Only when he doesn't get what he bargained for does he become aware of what he bargained for. Only on dissatisfaction does he dwell.....And that's dangerous, because the customer will be aware only of failure, of dissatisfaction, not of success or satisfaction. That makes him terribly susceptible to the blandishments of competitive sellers .... (g)etting customers for an intangible product requires the product to be tangibilised. ('The Marketing Imagination', Theodore Levitt. New York: The Free Press, 1986)

Such is not to minimalise or deny the importance of many central Church activities and programmes. Rather, it is to assert that in the need to secure new and increased finances, the local, tangible and parochial product is easier in terms of financial attraction.

However, there is another important and realistic issue to be acknowledged. With increasing costs for ministry, mission and maintenance, together with reduced congregations in the majority of parish churches, the local Church, having to give increasing amounts to the diocese and fund its own work and activities, will increasingly need to secure contributions from beyond the regular congregation. In many respects, this is not too difficult a task, but for many such requires a paradigmatic shift in marketing terms for the Church. The success or otherwise of such a strategy is not unconnected with the issue of perception and position. If the Church is perceived as giving added value to the community, there is a stronger possibility that the community will respond positively to Church appeals for resources. Some of the issues that Williams raises in respect of the Church of England still engaging with the community, both by its visible presence and the fact that many from beyond the congregation seek the ministry of the Church through baptism, marriage and funerals, provides the Church with a reservoir of potential donors and supporters. Other churches on mainland Europe enjoy wider community support through a Church tax, shared amongst various denominations on a proportionate basis. The Church of England, on the other hand, in spite of establishment, needs to secure the voluntary support from the wider community. Professor Richard Roberts describes the issue:

> ....*the national Churches of both Scotland and England display many of the sclerotic symptoms that mark nationalised industries: an all-embracing rhetoric of monopoly and service to the whole nation disguises an actual failure to discern the market and to prepare and deliver goods and services required by the customer in,*

or out of the pew. (Letter to the Independent newspaper, 17th May, 1991)

In order to secure sufficient resources and finance, the Church of England, if it is to remain truly the Church for the people of England, needs to look beyond congregations for support. Engagement in and with community projects and activities will secure community credibility. Imaginative and professional funding campaigns will place the Church alongside many other not-for-profit organisations who also seek voluntary contributions. The Church has often not found it too difficult to engender support for building and fabric purposes (this product is clearly tangible), but it now needs to convince the parish of its importance, contribution and significance to the life of the community that will enable non-Church people wanting to offer support. Given the significant and increasing turnover of resources in the average Parish Church, together with the required legislative accountability procedures, a more business-like approach and attitude is not only desirable but profoundly necessary. This will not be easy for those who by training, inclination and conviction see and experience the Church as distinct from the world of business and commerce.

A further area for consideration, not least in a world and culture where communication is so significant in the conveying of ideas and philosophies, is the need to keep both congregations and supporters informed about the Church's activities and message. All major charities provide regular information to supporters and would-be supporters in the form of professionally produced newsletters and magazines. A quarterly newsletter, for example, will not only provide regular information about the Church, but also circulate gifts, discounts at events, prize draw tickets and invitations to fundraising events. Potential and existing supporters will not necessarily know what is going on unless informed, and there is considerable competition in this market place. Parish web sites and regular articles through imaginative and professional press releases to local and national media will enable and enhance the visibility of the Church which, in turn, will make the securing of resources and finance an easier task.

Finally, Churches should be pro-active in seeking funds from major charitable trusts, grant making bodies and the National Lottery. Again, there is significant competition, but there are also significant sums of money to be drawn upon with the right approach and expertise. In some instances, the commissioning or employment of a consultant to undertake what is becoming a highly professional market could prove extremely worthwhile and potentially successful and rewarding. Many charities now use such people in their fundraising endeavours, and Churches who recognise the value of the parable of the talents (Matthew 25:14ff) should need little encouragement to engage in such an investment.

The issue of resources and finance for the work and mission of the Church of England, whilst more pressing and acute since the time of Bishop Williams, although there were even then indications of change, should not be one of total and complete despair. Resources and finances exist both within, but more critically beyond the local congregation. The latter may represent a diminishing return, but the market beyond is extensive, and the issue for the Church is knowing how best to secure significant sums for an important task and purpose. It is not difficult or beyond necessity for a cultural shift in attitude and approach. Perhaps Giles Fraser sums it up:

Without the discipline imposed by financial reality, shrinking churches are offered little incentive to change. Yes, richer churches must support poorer ones, and sacrificially so. No, redistribution of wealth must not be contingent on theology. But we need urgently to transform church culture and encourage initiative. ('Christianity with Attitude', Giles Fraser. Canterbury Press: Norwich, 2007)

iii) Doctrine and Grammar

The word "God" derives its meaning from within the complex patterns of religious reactions to the contingency of the world. To discuss what kind of reality this "God" has we must pay attention to those religious reactions. ('Wittgenstein, Grammar and God', Alan Keightley. Epworth Press, 1976)

For many, an increasing number, Christianity has become an unfamiliar language. Many people either do not know the words at all or, if they have heard the words, have no idea what they mean. ('Speaking Christian: Recovering the lost meaning of Christian words', Marcus J Borg. London: SPCK, 2011)

Bishop Williams acknowledged the difficulty many have with credal definitions and formulations. He was writing only three years after the publication of John Robinson's 'Honest to God', and there was still some sense both of the reality of God, however conceived, and the possibility of discourse about God. An earlier bishop had raised the issue in even more stark terms:

In March 1947 Bishop Barnes of Birmingham set out in "The Rise of Christianity" a theology that rejected the evidence of the Virgin Birth, the Miracles and the Resurrection. Over the next year his book sold more than 15,000 copies and generated a huge, wildly varied postbag. "It is such a brave book," the actress Sybil Thorndike wrote to him, "and coming from a priest of the Church it is more than brave. It has been a releasing for me, and I am sure it must have been for many people"('Austerity Britain 1945-51', David Kynaston. Bloomsbury, Publishing, 2007)

The Archbishop of Canterbury, Dr Geoffrey Fisher, explicitly disavowed Barnes, but a survey in the Sunday Pictorial requesting the views of its readers received more than three-quarters of a million in one week:

The upshot was a torrent of words.... With 52 per cent of letters supporting Barnes, 32 per cent against and the rest neutral. Tellingly, his opponents highlighted hypocrisy at least as much as doctrinal impurity. (ibid)

In 1966, however, there was still a grammar of God, and to use a concept from the later Wittgenstein, there was still a 'form of life' within which such language could be meaningfully engaged. Such cannot be assumed today. Not only are there competing theologies, as represented by differing faith traditions, but with increasing secularisation there can be no meaningful assumptions about the use of the word 'God', let alone any of the doctrines or dogmas associated with religious faith.

Many Christian churches have confessional documents or statements to which members are required to assent. The Church of England possesses no such foundational document, although it is acknowledged that authority derives from the scriptures, tradition and reason. Anglican clergy are required to give assent to the faith as revealed in the scriptures, catholic creeds, the Book of Common Prayer, the ordering of bishops, priests and deacons and the thirty nine articles of religion. The latter is the nearest the Church of England ever got to a distinctive confessional document, but the assent given is one of acknowledgement and has no binding authority. It is often asserted that Anglican belief is located in its liturgy, and as such it could be argued that there is a Wittgensteininian approach to meaning as that conveyed through the doing of worship, the form of life or language game.

The consequence of this, together with the breadth and tolerance associated with belief and doctrine exhibited within the Church of England, is that it is well placed to offer space for doctrines and creed to be explored openly and in an enquiring manner. Whilst there are some within the Church that would wish to close the debate, and assert a more rigid, often biblically based set of beliefs which would thereby become normative with little to no possibility of variation or deviation, there are many – perhaps a majority – who would encourage exploration and even modification of many traditionally assumed beliefs. Amongst the latter can be included the birth of Jesus to a virgin, the bodily resurrection of Jesus and even the literal divinity of Christ, as expressed within the doctrine of the Holy Trinity where Christ is represented as the eternal second person of the Godhead, equal in all respects with God the Father but at the same time possessing a full human nature. The Church of England has been able to incorporate both a highly conservative and biblically based theology together with, and alongside, a more liberal and critical outlook for many decades subsequent to the rise of biblical criticism from both perspectives and many in between. It has only been in recent years that the respective positions have become polarised and somewhat antagonistic, if not aggressive.

For many the debates about doctrine and dogma, including that of how the Bible can be interpreted, understood and used even in the twenty-first century, is very much an internal one to the life of the Church. It becomes focused when someone outside of the regular experience and life of the Church seeks baptism and Church membership, at least, that is, for the individual concerned. However, for the vast majority of people, namely those with little to no contact with the Church, the debate and the issues are of little concern, even if the grammar and language could be understood. The question for the Church in such a context is how does it speak of God in a way that can at the very least be heard, let alone understood. Reliance on traditional language and forms just will not suffice.

Grace Davie recounts a questionnaire:

Do you believe in God?' 'Yes.' Do you believe in a God who can change the course of events on earth?' 'No, just the ordinary one (from a study conducted in Islington in 1968 by Abercrombie et al. and quoted in 'Religion in Britain since 1945', Grace Davie.

43

Blackwell, 1994)

Davie poses the further question:

What is the significance, sociological or otherwise, of an <u>ordinary</u> God? Is this, or is it not, evidence of religious belief? If it is not belief, what kind of categories are necessary to understand this persistent dimension of British life and how would these relate to more orthodox dimensions of religiosity?(ibid)

Another sociologist, the Rev Dr Canon Alan Billings, identifies what he describes as 'cultural Christianity' as a way of understanding the 'ordinary God' of much popular belief:

We are a society that has been deeply influenced by the Christian religion and that will be true for a very long time to come ..... Britain is culturally Christian. This raises the interesting theological question of whether you can be Christian wholly outside of the Church. Members of churches, especially the clergy, would be horrified at such a suggestion; but many people in this country – as the census bears out – insist that they are Christians even though they never attend church. I think this means that sociologically we have to identify two types of Christianity now in Britain. On the one hand there are those who do attend churches – there is 'church Christianity'; on the other hand, there are those who live by Christian values and believe in God but who do not see the need to be in church every week or even at all – there is "cultural Christianity", the legacy of church Christianity. ('Secular Lives, Sacred Hearts', Alan Billings. SPCK, 2004)

Perhaps this is what Angela Tilby was alluding to when she wrote:

At the same time, the secularisation of religion in academic life and the media has not led to the exclusion of the sacred. The longing for the sacred continues to manifest itself in ordinary human language and speech and yearning, not only in the margins of life but in its very centre. There are still many believers, still many who pray, who look for God. It is just that, on Sunday, they have better things to do. ('Evangelism in an Age of Mass Media', Angela Tilby in 'Living Evangelism', ed. Jeffrey John. London: Darton, Longman and Todd, 1996).

Where, therefore, are the pressure points concerning possible meaningful discourse and debate about God and the Christian understanding of his/her nature? Furthermore, is such really a problem for the Church of England as it exists and ministers in the early twenty-first century?

There are few Christians, especially in a post 'Honest to God' age, that view God as a bearded old man inhabiting a wandering cloud somewhere in the stratosphere. The acceptance of such an anthropomorphic and physical deity is no longer sustainable, if it ever was. This does not prevent religious detractors from ascribing such a view to believers. The difficulty for the believer is what can meaningfully be substituted for the 'father in the sky' image? For some even to talk of the reality of God presents theological and philosophical difficulty. Reality presupposes existence, and existence assumes some form of spatial habitation. If God is real, in what sense is he/she real and where can the deity be located that in some way is transcendent to all other reality as experienced? The transcendence versus immanence of God is an old and familiar debate, but how can such be resolved to make the grammar or talk of God meaningful in any comprehendible and relevant sense? It is possible, of course, to recourse to language about God as Spirit or love, although both may do insufficient justice to the idea of God put forward by St Anselm in his Ontological Argument as that which nothing greater can be conceived of, and therefore the necessity of existence. The philosophy of existentialism perhaps permits a rather more practical way of talking about God, which is not just to do with reality and existence, but rather that which is expressed in everyday life by ordinary human beings, although perhaps in the more extraordinary moments of life. Such could reflect the disclosure situations articulated by Austin Farrer and Ian Ramsey, although perhaps better put by Sallie McFague when she writes:

> But what, more specifically, does our experiment say about the transcendence and immanence of God to and in the world? The central picture we have been developing is of the world as God's body, which God – and we – mother, love and befriend. God is incarnated or embodied in our world, in both cosmological and anthropological ways. The implication of this picture is that we never meet God unmediated or unembodied. The transcendence of God in our picture, whatever it does mean, cannot be understood apart from the world, or to phrase it more precisely, what we can know of God's transcendence is neither above nor beneath but in and through the world. We meet God in the body of the world….The world is our meeting place with God, and this means that God's immanence will be "universal" and God's transcendence will be "worldly". ('Models of God', Sallie McFague. SCM Press, 1987)

The Church of England may have a particular mission to develop language about God that is rooted, resonates and relevant to the everyday experiences of life. In this respect, the Church can build up and engage with those who Billings describes as 'cultural Christians' and whom the Church of England encounters more than many other churches. In particular, the Church should not be afraid to both lead and follow wherever this debate may lead, and not being a confessional Church is of some advantage and value. For the more sensitive, it could be acknowledged that the Judeo-Christian faith is rooted in a sense of journey, a wilderness and exilic experience, and a crucifixion and resurrection revelation. Put simply, the exploration, rather than being a betrayal of doctrines associated with and representing ideas of God, could well be the will of God.

The more detailed doctrines associated with the Christian revelation of God, whilst presenting many problems for contemporary thought and expression, may not in fact be too problematic for the Church if it does not feel the need to cling to what is considered biblical or theological literalism. It is perhaps worth noting that in respect of the virgin birth, the bodily resurrection, the divinity of Christ and the Trinity, none of the creeds are specific about the meaning or form of the doctrines. Clearly, each presents a problem if considered literally: virgins do not have babies, dead bodies do not become alive again, a fully human being cannot simultaneously possess the qualities of a fully divine being without betraying the integrity of either, and how can a unity be a trinity at the same time? Sermons can often address these problems with an appeal either to the omnipotence of God or to the unfathomable mystery surrounding what are described as revelations. Williams, as has been noted, was not unaware of these problems and clearly thought them worthy of consideration. Some would argue that to challenge or deny any or all of them is to desert the path of the Christian faith completely. Others may argue that they are not of the essence of the ministry of the rabbi from Nazareth, or the revelation of God in the Christ figure. It would not be appropriate in this work to give either a detailed affirmation or refutation of these issues. Such can easily and readily be found elsewhere. There are biblical problems concerning the use of the word 'virgin' in its Hebrew and Greek forms, there are conflicting accounts concerning the risen Christ and no account of a resurrection, there is nothing like the assertion of Jesus as God (a claim Jesus himself would have denied); that was to evolve outside of the New Testament period. Many early Christians, unfamiliar with early Greek philosophical thought would find a fully blown trinitarian doctrine at best incomprehensible, and at worst simply heretical. For the present purpose, given the acknowledged difficulty such doctrines, and many others, present, is whether the Church of England is able to embrace those who would want by inclination of conviction to adopt a metaphorical or mythical view of credal statements, together with those who would assert a more literal understanding or interpretation, without one side imposing its view or perception of orthodoxy upon the other? Hitherto, this has been the reality In the life of the Church of England, although such is subject to considerable pressure at the present time. The traditional inclusive nature of the Church should permit such a possibility, but the prominence of more tender souls presents a significant challenge. However, if the reality of God is worthy of consideration, should not his/her adherents be adventurous in seeking relevant and appropriate forms of grammar and doctrine to permit, facilitate and encourage the discourse? As the later Wittgenstein pointed out, and as the Church of England has practised, not least in its liturgical formulations, language can be used and understood in very different ways, but the way it is used and the context within which it is used contains, carries and conveys the meaning of what is being said:

> *Luther said that theology is the grammar of the word "God". I interpret this to mean that an investigation of the word would be a grammatical one. For example, people might dispute about how many arms God had, and someone might enter the dispute by denying that one could talk about arms of God. This would throw light on the use of the word. What is ridiculous or blasphemous also shows the grammar of the word. ('Wittgenstein's Lectures Cambridge 1932-1935', ed. Alice Ambrose. Blackwell: Oxford, 1979)*

Fergus Kerr reminds us that language, including language about God, can only be attended to within the context of the signs of our lives within the world as lived and experienced:

Theology as grammar is, then, the patient and painstaking description of how, when we have to, we speak of God. But why is it that we doubt it can be in mere words or signs or bodily activities that we discover anything interesting about our inner selves or about the divine? Why is it that we are so strongly tempted to turn away from what we say and do, as if these were not "significant" enough? Again and again Wittgenstein reminds us that we have no alternative to attending to the signs, the repertoire of gestures and so on that interweave our existence. We have no access to our own minds, non-linguistically. We have no access to the divine, independently of our life and language. It goes against the grain, so captivated are we by the metaphysical tradition, but Wittgenstein keeps reminding us of the obvious fact: we have nothing else to turn to but the whole complex system of signs which is our human world. ('Theology after Wittgenstein', Fergus Kerr. Blackwell: Oxford, 1986)

A further area of issue in respect of understanding the doctrine and grammar of God within the Church, as it impacts upon the majority of non-Churchgoing people, is that of the persistence of evil and suffering in the world. Furthermore, there is that of the activity of prayer seeking the intervention of the deity to effect a change in events or to put things right on behalf of the one or ones who pray. If there was one significant point at which the grammar of God is most problematic it is the experience of suffering when correlated with the existence of a loving and omnipotent deity, together with the fact of apparently unanswered prayer to obtain relief and effect an observable good. It has been cynically suggested that the verb 'to pray' means:

.....to ask that the laws of the universe be annulled on behalf of a single petitioner confessed unworthy. ('The Enlarged Devil's Dictionary', Ambrose Bierce. Victor Gollancz, 1967)

In spite of Bierce's cynicism, a theological problem arises when petitions are to all appearances either ignored or refused. When the earnest petitions to a loving creator and sustainer to effect some good, or prevent evil, by an array of manifestly devout believers are ignored, questions must be raised concerning both the nature and the power of God. Ivan Karamazov's protest is one that cannot be ignored:

And if the sufferings of children go to make up the sum of sufferings which is necessary for the purchase of truth, then I say beforehand that the entire truth is not worth such a price .....It is not God that I do not accept .....I merely most respectfully return him the ticket. ('The Brothers Karamazov, Volume 1', Fyodor Dostoyevsky. Penguin Books: Middlesex, 1958)

Classical theism has defined certain attributes of God which God, by definition, would need to possess to be God. Amongst these is the omnipotence of God: God can do anything. Furthermore, the Church has traditionally taught that God used his omnipotence to create the universe and has, from time to time, intervened in the operation of the same to bring about a change which might otherwise have not occurred. This is not the place to consider a detailed examination of the origin of the universe and God's involvement in the same, but, rather to point to a profound and significant difficulty that the Church has in proclaiming a God who appears to many to be either arbitrary, unconcerned or impotent. As Paul Davies has pointed out, there are significant confusions in respect of a necessary God creating the universe:

Christians, like all monotheists, believe in <u>one</u> God. So they need to *show not only that God exists necessarily, but that this being is necessarily unique – otherwise there could be countless necessary beings making countless universes. Even if all of this can be sorted out, we are still confronted with the problem that, in spite of God's necessary existence and nature, God did <u>not necessarily</u> create the universe as it is, but instead merely <u>chose</u> to do so. But now the alarm bells ring. Can a necessary being act in a manner that is not necessary? Does that make sense?*

On the face of it, it doesn't. If God is necessarily as God is, then God's choices are necessarily as they are, and the freedom of choice evaporates. Nevertheless, there is a long history of attempts to get round this obstacle and to reconcile a necessary God with a contingent universe. ('The Goldilocks Enigma', Paul Davies. Penguin: London, 2006)

Our question is whether the Church of England is able to facilitate and enable a debate about the nature of God and his/her relation to the universe and humankind?

There are clear limits to the use of the word omnipotence as an attribute of God. Wittgenstein alluded to such when posing the question concerning the arms of God. More recently, the late D Z Phillips has pointed out logical inconsistencies with how the word omnipotence is used and understood:

The challenge to God's omnipotence would now take the following form:

1 *To say that God is omnipotent is to say that God can do anything describable in any practice without contradiction.*

2 *There are countless activities in different practices, describable there without contradiction, which God cannot do.*

There God is not omnipotent. If this is to be the test of God's omnipotence, isn't it clear that God fails the test? Here are just some activities within practices, describable without contradiction, which are part of the successful challenge: riding a bicycle, licking and savouring a Haagen-Dazs ice-cream, bumping one's head, having sexual intercourse, learning a language and so on and so on. ('The Problem of Evil and the Problem of God', D Z Phillips. SCM Press: London, 2004)

Whilst it can be argued that the above quotation represents a playing with words, it could also be said that all discourse is of this nature. Not only should we be careful in respect of the way we use language, but also be mindful of both its limitations and the reality or truth of any proposition that we may be attempting to convey in words. For the present purpose, in spite of the linguistic problems associated with the use of the 'omnipotent' in respect of God, there is the theological issue as to the validity of ascribing any understanding of omnipotence to a benevolent deity. One of the drivers and perhaps justification for religious belief is that there is a God who can do things, who can change things, who can make a difference. But as we have seen such presents a logical problem, not only of language but of consistency. In theological terms, such is described as the issue of theodicy: how can a loving, caring and compassionate God, possessing the power and ability to act and change things, not do so on occasions to prevent profound and significant human suffering? Could not God, being omniscient as well as omnipotent, have redirected the tsunami of Boxing Day, 2005 just a little to prevent such devastation and the loss of life that was inflicted upon so many people? There is also the related issue of people's perception of God's action, when there is an apparent personal benefit. A recent accident in the Dolomite region of Northern Italy, when an American fighter plane collided with a cable car plunging a number of people to a horrific death illicit a television comment from the next passenger who would have boarded the cable car, 'someone up there must have been looking after me.'

It is possible from within the context of the specifically

Christian revelation of and insight into God to argue for a powerless God, thereby by-passing the theodicy problem. Why should it be that religious believers ascribing ultimate value and meaning to God have to understand and proclaim such in imperialistic and powerful terms? In spite of the attempts of New Testament writers, editors and subsequent theologians to assert acts of power to the human Jesus of Nazareth, a more careful examination of the foundation texts and common sense application to the Christian story, the rabbi from Nazareth is perhaps better portrayed and affirmed as of a humble disposition than the redactors have written. Could it not be that such is God's nature, a real incarnation, and which would sit more comfortably with the most precise and definitive description of God as love and recorded in the first letter of John (1John 4)? Furthermore, the crucifixion and death of Christ represents the crucifixion and death of the presence of God in Christ, and there can be no more poignant portrayal of powerlessness than the suffering and dying of the crucified, and in whom the followers of Jesus saw and experienced the reality of God. Such is the Christian model and understanding of God. Jurgen Moltmann expressed it as follows:

> But the crucified God renounces these privileges of an idol. He breaks the spell of the super-ego which men lay upon him because they need this self-protection. In humbling himself and becoming flesh, he does not accept the laws of this world, but takes up suffering, anxious man into his situation. In becoming weak, impotent, vulnerable and mortal, he frees man from the quest for powerful idols and protective compulsions and makes him ready to accept his humanity, his freedom and his mortality. ('The Crucified God', Jurgen Moltmann. SCM Press: London, 1974)

However, the weakness and powerlessness of God as described by Moltmann cannot be one that is dipped into and out of at the divine will. Such would make no sense and would point to the duplicity if not disinguity of God. The weakness and power-lessness of the vulnerable God is more forcibly and poignantly expressed in the moving account of his experience in Auschwitz by Rabbi Elie Wiesel:

> *The three victims mounted together on to the chairs. The three necks were placed at the same moment within the nooses. "Long live liberty!" cried the two adults. But the child was silent. "Where is God? Where is He?" someone behind me asked. At a sign from the head of the camp, the three chairs tipped over.... Then the march past began. The two adults were no longer alive... But the third rope was still moving; being so light, the child was still alive..... Behind me, I heard the same man asking: "Where is God now?" And I heard a voice within me answer him:*
>
> *"Where is He? Here He is – He is hanging here on this gallows...."('Night', Elie Wiesel. Fontana Books: London, 1972)*

More recently, the Rev Canon Dr Giles Fraser has written:

> *But this [God's promise] does not offer the Christian worldview unlimited protection from the stormy blast of the tsunami. Christians cannot go on speaking about prayer as if it were an alter-native way of getting things done in the world, or about divine power as if God were the puppet master of the universe. What is so terrifying about the Christmas story is that it offers us nothing but the protection of a vulnerable baby, of a God so pathetic that we need to protect him. The idea of an omnipotent God who can calm the sea and defeat our enemies turns out to be a part of that great fantasy of power that has corrupted the Christian imagination for centuries. Instead, Christians are called to recognize that the essence of the divine being is not power but compassion and love. (ibid)*

If the Church of England is to engage effectively and credibly the issue of God with the people of the nation, it will have to incorporate contemporary philosophical, scientific and popular difficulties associated with such an engagement. The retreat into a ghetto of supposed theological and biblical orthodoxy or purity is not a realistic or honest option and will only result in increased alienation and marginalisation. The Church of England owes the people more in terms of the exploration and meaning of the grammar of God in the twenty-first century, and which may require the significant re-appraisal and re-interpretation of previously held doctrines, all of which have been through a process of change and amendment, and had a particular philosophical and historical context functioning within a 'form of life'. The warning from Chris Hedges in a review of Christopher Hitchens' book, 'God is Not Great: The Case Against Religion' is relevant:

> *Those who transform faith into a creed transplant religion into a profane rather than a sacred context. Like all idol-worshippers, they seek to give the world a unity and coherence it does not possess. And with this false coherence imposed, faith withers. ('False Gods' by Chris Hedges. New Statesman, 4th June, 2007)*

A further critique of the way that creeds function has been given by Steven Shakespeare and Hugh Rayment-Pickard:

> *.....the Church has in various ways tried to close down the debate about Jesus. The Church has tried to compensate for the lack of doctrinal certainty in the New Testament by providing various creeds that attempt to nail down the fluid and complex revelation of scripture. Creeds can be religiously useful as a foil to debate, or as stepping stones to a more exploratory faith .....It is easy to forget that the process of putting creeds together was itself a historical and human one full of debate and politics....Creeds, after all, are not definitions. They are summaries of larger stories, guides to reading*

those stories without trying to dispel all mystery from them, or forcing them into a narrow ideological explanation. ('The Inclusive God: Reclaiming Theology for an Inclusive Church', Steven Shakespeare and Hugh Rayment-Pickard. Canterbury Press Norwich, 2006)

In a review in the New Statesman magazine, Bishop Richard Holloway identifies how religious discourse, the grammar that people of faith use and communicate with is all too easily denying of the essential mystery which we call God. He writes:

In religious discourse, we too quickly move from the illuminating suggestions of parable, metaphor and myth into quasi-scientific claims about the nature of the mystery that we are hunting. The irony here is that religions end up doing to the elusive person of God what biological determinism does to the elusive person of the human: they void it of mystery. This is why intransigents on both sides of the current debate about God increasingly sound like each other. (Review of 'The Face of God: the Gifford Lecture', Roger Scruton, by Richard Holloway. The New Statesman, 2nd April, 2012)

Our doctrine and grammar need to recapture this essential mystery in a non-dogmatic form that ensures and enables access to the ultimate source of being and ultimate concern. The Church of England is in a good place to facilitate this encounter.

iv) Worship and Outreach

Worship is in fact central to the corporate life of the Church. It is above all in assembling together for prayer that we identify ourselves as believers...... It is in meeting for worship that the Church is made visible as a public and corporate entity ('The Praises of God', Mark Santer in 'Liturgy for a New Century', ed. Michael Perham. SPCK: London, 1991)

.....there is an integrated feel about Anglican liturgy which has

its origins in the union of heart and mind, of word and sacrament, of text and ceremonial. Our worship is earthed in a theology which is incarnational, and a sacramentality which is organic and affirmative. We belong in a tradition which retains strong echoes of the Benedictine pattern, with its emphasis on ordered worship, serious study and common life. While the English cathedrals, for example, consciously reflect this inheritance, it is true also of the parochial ministry, where the parsonage house is not only of prayer, but of study and hospitality. Our liturgy is ordered, not regimented, and it is related to how we think and how we live. ('Is there an "Anglican" liturgical style?', David S Stancliffe in 'The Identity of Anglican Worship', ed. Kenneth Stevenson and Bryan Spinks. Mowbray: London, 1991)

Worship is what Christians do and what the Church offers. The liturgy of the Church of England, not least since the time of the first Prayer Book of 1549, has been a significant part of English social and political life. As Bishop Williams noted, what the Church of England is, and what is believed is vividly expressed and demonstrated in its liturgy and not in any confessional document. Furthermore, the Church of England in its liturgy, and in spite of significant changes, not only in the period 1549 to 1662, but even in later times to our own day, has always professed to be both catholic and reformed. The Church of England retains a formal liturgy at its core, with recognisably catholic elements, but expressed in a reformed style and embracing both catholic and reformed theology and ecclesiology.

Bishop Williams identified a changing pattern of worship in the Church of England where the Parish Communion replaced the traditional 8.00 am Communion and the 11.00 am Matins pattern, that had prevailed for centuries as the familiar and mainstay of parochial worship. Many older members of Church congregations still value or long for this pattern. However, the change was welcomed not only because of the possibility of a more regular communicant life, but also greater involvement and participation by families. This has been sustained over the 46 years since Williams wrote his book, although there are notable exceptions to the format.

However, there have been many changes and developments since the Reformation, and more especially over the past 46 years. In 1966 the predominant form would have been the 1662 Book of Common Prayer, often with amendments and additions from the unauthorised and aborted 1928 revision, and which, in the most part, was incorporated into what became known as Series 1, which was authorised in 1966. The language of this rite, however, was distinctly Prayer Book, as was the subsequent revision in 1967, Series 2, although with a much lighter touch. This revision consciously attempted to reconstruct what was considered the early fourfold pattern and structure to the eucharistic rite of taking, blessing, breaking and giving. It was not until Series 3 was authorised in 1973 that the language of the liturgy became more contemporary, and was the first service to address God as 'you' rather than 'thou'. The authorised Alternative Service Book of 1980 (ASB) was a natural development from Series 3, and offered services in both so-called traditional (Rite B) and contemporary language (Rite A), together with a range of different eucharistic prayers. Although only authorised for ten years, its life was prolonged by a further ten to enable the approval, acceptance and production of the liturgical book Common Worship, with further variety and options, thereby enabling a rich menu of options for worship in the increasing variety of styles in English Parish Churches. As well as eight eucharistic prayers, the provision of services according to the Book of Common Prayer and seasonal provisions for use within the Eucharist, Common Worship has effected a major revision of the other services of the Church, including the rites concerning baptism, marriage and funerals.

This is not the place for a detailed examination of the history and development of worship within the Church of England. Rather, it is relevant to the subject in hand to consider the impact of liturgical change upon the life of the Church, and the importance of such for the outreach of the Church and its engagement with wider society. It is clear that the principle of uniformity of worship cannot be maintained with the variety and options now on offer, if ever really were the case. The days of a single worship book, in the form of the Book of Common Prayer, supplemented by a hymn book, are long past, and no amount of liturgical nostalgia and lobbying by the Prayer Book Society will see the return of widespread use of a book that has contributed so much to the development of the English language, and has been so closely identified with the faith of the English. It is to be seen whether Common Worship, which has improved the grammar and style exhibited in the ASB, will become equally as well bedded in the life of the Church of England. There are signs that congregations are coming to value not only the style of Common Worship, but also the variety it offers, thereby enriching the worship in the ordinary Parish Church. The further resource book, Times and Seasons, provides for further enrichments for the major seasons and festivals of the Church.

For those outside of the life of the Church, or the occasional attendee, the loss of the Prayer Book is not an issue, as they were probably not even aware of its existence. Some, however, may have been familiar with bits of it having experienced such on the odd occasions. Its continued use or promotion is unlikely to encourage or enthuse many to attend Church on a regular basis, although there may be some appreciation of the beauty of the language and cadences. Liturgical scholarship has moved on considerably over the past 46 years, and not only in respect of the historical roots and origins of the liturgy. Liturgists, often despised by more traditional elements in the Church, are equally concerned about the impact and relevance of what is said and sung in Church, both for the regular worshipper and that person who, for whatever reason, has made that most difficult of journeys across the Church threshold, and through the imposing, if not restricting Church door. What greets them in addition to the sidespeople, who may be handing out a proliferation of literature, which may or may not make any sense to the wandering soul, is the liturgy. Furthermore, this will not just be the words or music that impact upon the visitor but also the style and presentation. Such will include accessibility to the words and actions. In this respect the literature and its format are of crucial importance to enable an understanding of what is going on and facilitate some form of meaningful participation. Many Churches, therefore, produce their own service booklets, which can vary according to the different times during the Church's year. Whilst it is important to observe the changing seasons of the year, which evoke an emotional sense of movement and experience, it is also desirable to use the variety of words and music to reflect more adequately the liturgical engagement. Human beings are creatures with feelings, and such should be engaged and touched by the liturgical action. This is at its most obvious through the major seasons and festivals of the Church. D H Lawrence summed this up:

> *The rhythm of life itself was preserved by the Church hour by hour, day by day, season by season, year by year, epoch by epoch, down among the people, and the wild coruscations were accommodated to this permanent rhythm. We feel it, in the south, in the country, when we hear the jangle of the bells at dawn, at noon, at sunset, marking the hours with the sound of mass or prayers. It is the rhythm of the daily sun. We feel it in the festivals, the procession, Christmas, the Three Kings, Easter, Pentecost, St John's day, All Saints, All Souls. This is the wheeling of the year, the movement of the sun through solstice and equinox, the coming of the seasons, the going of the seasons. And it is the inward rhythm of man and woman, too, the sadness of Lent, the delight of Easter, the wonder of*

Pentecost, the fires of St John, the candles on the graves of All Souls, the lit-up tree of Christmas, all representing kindled rhythmic emotions in the souls of men and women. And men experience the great rhythm of emotion man-wise, women experience it woman-wise, and in the unison of men and women it is complete. ('Apropos of Lady Chatterley's Lover', D H Lawrence. Heinemann: London, 1969)

Worship has to engage people not only with the raising of the spirit to the divine within the beauty and inspiration through what is offered, but also a profound sense of relevance to the lives of people in the community. If it does not touch people at the point of their aspirations, hopes and even fears, then worship runs the serious risk of being an act of self-indulgence by those responsible for its performance, lay and ordained. Similarly, there needs to be opportunity for engagement with what is happening in the liturgy, although not as much as some churches think is necessary or desirable. The movement of worship should enable adoration and reflection, as well as the participation of those present, whether as individuals or as represented by others. At its best, worship is dynamic and participatory, and there is the need to ensure that it is never dominated by one or just a few devotees. Within the context of the Eucharistic liturgy, the president of the rite should, at certain times, 'disappear' as others exercise their rightful and representative functions within the act. For example, the presiding minister should not invite the people to confess their sins, read lessons, proclaim the Gospel, lead the prayers of the faithful, invite the people to share the peace, invite the acclamation in the anaphora, affirm the fraction and dismiss the people. Such acts belong either to the deacon, as the 'bridge' person or representatives of the people. Where this dynamic is evidenced and experienced the worshipper, whether regular or casual, witnesses an act that is done for and with the people of the community. This is outreach and enables participation, rather than just being a spectator to a ritual.

What happens and what is said within the liturgy is clearly important and significant. Sermons have often been criticised, if not ridiculed, either for length, incomprehensibility or irrelevance. There are many examples of the preacher reading a text which he/she may have prepared based upon the readings or the season sometime during the preceding week, or occasionally the previous year from the file labelled 'sermons', and which do not touch any contemporary event, issue or crisis. In this sense, the sermon is merely an exposition or commentary upon the readings or some associated doctrine of the Church. Such may be very enlightening, and possibly enriching, but is it performing the function of enabling insight and facilitating thought and challenge to the world and life as experienced by the captive audience as represented by the congregation? For some, length is a virtue and indicative of study and time spent on preparation with very little question as to whether the time could have been better spent. In an age when the soundbite or the newspaper headline is arresting and catching immediate communication, should the sermon be of lecture room type covering as many different aspects of the subject matter as possible? In an age when there was nothing else to do on Sunday, to spend up to an hour listening to the vicar's sermon represented a good way of whiling away the dull hours of a dull day. Such is no longer the case, but nevertheless people still seek some insight to the issues which confront society and themselves, and furthermore from a religious and spiritual perspective. However, such needs to be engaging (but not trite and patronising) and relevant. If the Gospel, the good news, is not engaging and relevant to those who hear and experience it, then it is nothing at all. There is clearly an art and skill in such communication, and perhaps more attention should be given to appropriate training. Good, short, interesting, relevant and sometimes amusing sermons will capture the attention of the hearer, and especially those who may not have experienced such before or may be attending Church for the first time either ever or in a long time. Comfort and warmth are contemporary necessities, and the Church can no longer afford to delude itself that people will attend no matter how cold or how painful is the experience. Attention to these details is as important as attending to the formalities of the liturgy. This is outreach, and the liturgy is the Church's prime evangelistic methodology as this is what we do as our core and prime activity.

The Church of England possesses a structured and agreed liturgy with significant flexibility and variation, as now permitted within the Common Worship texts. It is still assumed, however, that churches will use the prescribed forms and adapt the same to suit local contexts and situations. It is often mistakenly thought that those outside the Church would find a formal text and form off-putting and difficult. This is not true as people attending Church for the first time or after a significant lapse, value knowing where they are and what is happening. It is often the regular churchgoer who seeks a less structured form to suit him/herself. However, the need for a form that people can follow raises the accessibility issue, in terms of the words being used or spoken. Equally important are details concerning posture, actions and movement. The Book of Common Prayer, whilst being familiar to most churchgoers in past years, is one of the least accessible of books for those with little to no knowledge or experience of the worship of the Church. Clearly, the literature provided for the worshipper needs to be tailor-made to what is going to happen and will, therefore, have a local dimension. No centrally produced book or leaflet can provide this, and Common Worship envisaged the production of local forms, albeit with appropriate copyright acknowledgement. The worship book needs to be clear and precise so that there is a minimum of interruption, if any, from the worship leader about what is occurring, or what is to happen. Most people can read straightforward texts and do not need patronising by the clergy! Consideration needs also to be given to those who are visually impaired and require larger type. Even the use of hymn books is questionable, containing often in excess of 600 hymns when only 4 or 5 are going to be used, and the temptation to burden the worshipper with a library of literature should be resisted, no matter how important the vicar may think it all is! If our worship is not ordered, offered or presented in a way that enables those attending, whether regular or otherwise, to feel both uplifted and challenged, then the Church is guilty of failing to present the Gospel requirement to worship God in Christ, and to be enthused to serve his/her people. Worship can be the gateway to faith and not necessarily the other way round. It was the great preacher and teacher, John Wesley, who reminds us that all the Communion service can be a converting ordinance!

Bishop Williams perceived the significant liturgical changes that were already occurring in 1966 and which were to proceed at a pace not dissimilar to those of the immediate post-reformation time. He acknowledged the value and importance of these changes and recognised that such were necessary within the context of a changing social environment. However, he was able to write:

> *God must be as near to us in the home, factory, or office as in church. But are we as near to Him? Do we not need the times of refreshing in the conscious presence of the Lord? Do we not need to put away for a time the clamour of secular concerns, in order to fix our minds on that which is eternal? Do we not need the inspiration of fellowship with others in sacrament, prayer and meditation? .....The Church has given answers to these questions for nearly twenty centuries. Those who think that a few scientific discoveries, a few changes in social habit and an increased knowledge of psychology have invalidated the Church's long experience and opened up a totally new way to God have undertaken to prove a very daring*

thesis. I shall be surprised if they succeed in doing so(ibid)

v) Occasional Offices

As a nation we have largely stopped attending church: in that sense this is a time of no religion and we lead secular lives. But we have not ceased to be spiritual beings and we are still influenced by the Christian legacy: most of us are "cultural Christians" – we still have sacred hearts. The Church has a choice: it can continue to be the Church of the nation by trying to keep that legacy alive or it can turn its back by turning inward and becoming one more religious sect along the high street. Opportunities for renewing the Christian legacy occur when the ministry of the Church is sought. This happens at baptisms, weddings and funerals, and when people in a particular place and in certain circumstances become aware of themselves as a community and turn to the Church for specific ministry. ('Secular Lives, Sacred Hearts' by Alan Billings. SPCK: London, 2004)

The baby crying may well be doing so at a hole-in-the-corner baptism, on a Sunday afternoon, the congregation exclusively family and friends. The local pastor has perhaps been pressurized into presiding at such a service by influential people who may only come to church once a year, if that. There is an impressive array of Sunday hats. The baby may even be late for its own baptism because the limousine couldn't get there on time. Pastor and church door-keeper stand at the entrance to the church, silently seething as yet one more exercise in consumer-religion seems to be about to take place. The photo-call after the service is over is lengthy. The pastor has already had a grueling Sunday morning, in the course of which he has preached three times in three different places. All he wants to do is go home, put his feet up and rest – before his fourth sermon, at Evensong. ('The First Rites' by Kenneth Stevenson. Lamp Press: London, 1989)

These two quotations represent two contrasting views concerning the administration of what are known as the occasional offices. Both views are held, often strongly, within the Church of England today. The occasional offices are those services determined by the occasion, and are not part of the regular weekly or daily services undertaken in the Parish Church. In one sense, they occur 'on demand' by an individual, a couple, a family or an organisation. In the main they comprise the services of Holy Baptism, Holy Matrimony and Funeral/Burial, although others would include Confirmation, Visitation of the Sick, Penance, thanksgiving for a child or after a birth, memorial services, civic services or others. Almost by definition such services are consumerist in that there is a consumer with a need or request.

The occasional offices, therefore, are those services through which the Church comes into contact with and provides for those not always, if at all, who form part of the regular congregation. Furthermore, what is clear is that in spite of a reduction in the number of these services and of those occurring in Church, given other venues such as hotels or castles, there is still very much a demand, and that demand is largely concentrated within the Church of England. In 2009, the Church of England baptised 138,300 people which represented a decrease of only 840 from the previous year ('The Church of England Year Book', Church House Publishing: London, 2012). The figures for the comparable year in respect of marriages and funerals were 52,730 and 176,660, respectively. The dilemma for the Church and clergy is, therefore, twofold: the physical ability to conduct such services given a declining number of available stipendiary clergy, and the need to conduct the same with some degree of integrity whilst being open and responsive to where people are coming from and what they expect. The integrity and responsiveness can be dissonant with each other, at the very least.

There is something very Church of England about these

services. Apart from the legal requirement placed upon the parish priest to baptise, marry or bury any of his/her parishioners, there resides an expectation within the parish that people can call upon the Church to conduct the same, even if they do not attend Church or support it financially. There is a strong view within parishes that somehow the Church of England, like any other public institution or provision, not only exists to be used when required, but is also resourced by the state. It exists rather like a public library or a museum, only making a minimal charge for the services. Even if it is recognised that the Church is not funded by the state, many convince themselves, in spite of evidence to the contrary, that the Church of England is very wealthy, especially in respect of land and property, and can well afford to fund itself. Father Robert Doherty, S.J., Professor at Pope John XXIII National College, has described the increasing tendency to view Churches as 'Religious Museums': 'everyone wants to have a museum in their community. But no-one visits the museum every week, and few expect to be involved. Rather, the museum is a place where people go two or three times a year – to look and enjoy.'

Whilst this perspective on Church finances is deeply embedded in English culture, and is something with historic roots in that in the not too distant past, the local Church was resourced in a number of ways which did not impact upon the congregation or the local community, there is a growing consumer awareness that 'you get what you pay for'. In respect of the sacrament of marriage, where the average cost of a wedding now exceeds £20,000, there is much that the Church could offer that could easily compete with any hotel, castle or whatever. However, such would require a degree of professional presentation and marketing that is not familiar with many clergy or parishes. Realistic charges for what amounts to the use of a Church building and setting, to say nothing of the affable, willing and receptive priest, would not necessarily diminish the significance and solemnity of the occasion, but rather could be the source of many seeking a Church wedding as opposed to other venues. Most of the latter seek to imitate the Church setting and ambience. Why not, therefore, offer the real thing and enable those seeking the setting to hear gently the theology of marriage and be allowed to make a realistic contribution to the maintenance and continuation of the parish church? Follow up invitations to continue to support the Church where the marriage has taken place ensures a continued link and relationship.

Baptism is the sacrament of initiation into the Church and should, therefore, be taken very seriously. However, this does not mean that it should not be accessible and welcoming to those who make an enquiry often for what is called 'a christening'. The making of the request, however understood, or seen perhaps just as a rite of passage, is indicative of an intention which the Church should not decry or denigrate. It is unfortunate that the National Curriculum teaches baptism as a rite of passage, which could lead potential parents to see it just as that. A welcome and encouragement from the parish priest, together with information, literature and possible meeting(s) enable families to experience the Church and parish priest as people who rejoice at the request and want to support, and not merely to 'get them in on our terms'. There is no substitute to resourcing this work and pastoral visiting of those families seeking baptism. The rite itself should be celebrated within the eucharistic context of the Church's life, thereby enabling families to see and experience the goal of Church membership as communicants within the Body of Christ. Such also enables the regular congregation to evidence a welcome to fellow parishioners who may never have experienced eucharistic worship which, as Wesley rightly said, is a converting ordinance. The administration of the sacrament of Holy Baptism is a precious gift of and to the Church and which is openly and lovingly offered to all parishioners. For all the talk and ideas of new ways of engaging with people, baptism remains the point at which contact is not only most easily made, but which is initiated by many who are outside the regular life of the Church. Follow-up visits, anniversary cards, invitations to events and possible regular support of the Church often produce positive responses from those who have been engaged positively. Such has not changed in the forty years since Bishop Williams wrote:

> 't must be remembered that to offer Baptism to all children may be much closer to the basic idea of the Gospel than to impose tests. Christ laid great stress on the <u>indiscriminate</u> goodness of God – "He maketh his sun to rise on the evil and on the good, and sendeth rain on the just and on the unjust." Baptism, even indiscriminate Baptism, would express this unconditional love and mercy of God for all far better than Baptism administered on the strength of some righteous performance, either on the part of the candidate or his family. (ibid)

Writing some 22 years later, the Bishop of Winchester, Dr John Taylor wrote concerning the Baptism service for his gardener's son:

> For him the drinking of the champagne and the cutting of the cake were just as much a part of the ritual as the sprinkling of the water. That was for him a rather strange part, he could understand the rest. The point was that the Church has always assumed that Baptism is <u>its</u> ritual which it can dispense to those who seem to be qualified for it, but which it certainly has to explain. I came to see that what we are asked to perform is <u>their</u> ritual, and if we are prepared to do that as one of the still surviving rituals of our society, then we can claim the right to say, "can we tell you what we see in this?" and to explain the deeper Christian understanding of that ritual.
>
> ('Conversion to the World', John Taylor in 'The Parish Church', edited by Giles Ecclestone. A R Mowbray & Co., Oxford, 1988)

Alan Billings warns of the danger of not being open and responsive to where people are in their lives and requests for baptism:

> *The price we pay is that we lose contact with a large proportion of the non-churchgoing but Christian population at this crucial moment in their lives – the birth of a child – and fail to nourish and educate their faith. But there is a connection between baptism understood in this way and mission. What is being displayed at every baptism is the relevance of Christian faith to mundane concerns, such as the successful raising of children. Infant baptism is one of those increasingly rare occasions when Christians can demonstrate that they do not think of themselves – in Bonhoeffer's striking image – as travelling in a sealed train through enemy territory(ibid)*

Appropriate emphasis and training on baptism preparation and practice for priests and parishes could prove to be a more effective mission strategy than other more recently devised programmes which bear little relationship to the historic Church, a contemporary ecclesiology and an integrity that engages with people from where they are and what they seek. The administration of the sacrament of baptism is still a right thing to do.

In spite of a significant increase in the number of couples living together, or as some would describe co-habiting, thereby avoiding the pejorative 'living in sin', marriage is still a popular activity and way of living. It should be acknowledged, however, that there is a trend for people to get married later in life, often having lived together for a period, and also a significant rise in the number of divorces and subsequent marriage. The position of the Church of England is that any person has a right to be married in their parish church, defined either geographically or by virtue of membership on the Church Electoral Roll, signifying regular attendance, subject to any impediment. The parish priest does not have to marry a couple where one party has a former marriage partner who is still alive, although he/she has the discretion to conduct the ceremony if certain conditions can be met, or not, as the case may be. This may be the position if marriage between couples of the same gender is permitted and made legal. A Church wedding, often described and thought of as 'traditional', is still the aspiration of many and such should be encouraged by a Church wishing to assist in the fulfillment of the hopes and aspirations of parishioners, whether Church attenders or not. As with baptism, there are significant opportunities to meet and engage with people who may not otherwise have much contact or involvement with the Church. The Church does not have to seek these potential 'customers'; they present themselves and should be made welcome. This is in spite of the resources they may bring!

Weddings are becoming increasingly professional occasions. There are many professional people involved, including wedding planners, photographers, video people, cars, dressmakers, printers, etc. Many present themselves at Wedding Fayres, and the use of the internet is an increasing resource for couples arranging their wedding, with all the attendant problems that sites with American origins can present. If the Church is serious about its wishes to continue to offer what for many is either a sacrament or a solemn religious occasion, then it needs to be professional in presenting what it offers. Clearly, there is a pastoral opportunity and necessity to engage with those getting married and attending to any difficulties, some of which may be personal and familial. There is nothing like a wedding to induce problems and tensions, some of which may have a historic pedigree! Many weddings now have a designer feel, and it is important to be flexible in respect of a couple's requirements and wishes. Such, of course, would have to be consistent with the authorised liturgy of the Church, but there is considerable opportunity for innovation and variation. This is often welcomed and sometimes unexpected. It is also time consuming, but a favourable reaction to the priest and Church in their endeavours to provide the best for that special day secures a positive response to the Church in a climate and culture that is often negative and critical, even if without justification. The mission opportunities are not about getting couples 'into' the Church but, rather, that of meeting people where they are and addressing needs, hopes and aspirations.

It is important, however, that couples getting married in Church are made aware of what the ceremony is about, and what they are expected to say before both God and witnesses. This is not the same as what is often described as marriage preparation, which is often not necessary given the nature of contemporary relationships and patterns of living. Simple leaflets in a Church pack of information will often suffice and permit questions. A customised parish wedding pack can contain much helpful information for the preparation of a wedding. As well as detailing all the Church costs, there can be information about additional services the Church might offer in respect of bells, choir, soloists and flowers, together with related costs. Other information could include suggestions for hymns and readings, thereby obviating the need for the internet. Advertisements for reception venues, wedding cars, photographers, printers, etc. can also be a revenue source, both for the production of a professional pack and the Church. Above all, however, is the availability and accessibility of the priest or designated person to help and assist in the planning and preparation to ensure a memorable day and occasion. As with baptism such can produce results in terms of a positive view of the Church, and thereby the Christian faith than might otherwise have been the case. There is the additional possibility of continued and regular financial support for the Church. Alan Dillings reminds us that:

People want to get married in a church because it is a "sacred place"..... A place is sacred because it is associated with serious and significant events in the life of a person or their family.....Being married in this place, which is sacred for them, is part of what I mean by cultural Christianity..... Instead of moaning and complaining, priests and congregations should rejoice that so many people understand themselves to be Christian and seek their sacred place for the various rites of passage. (Ibid)

To conduct a funeral service, whether in Church or at a crematorium can be one of the most demanding aspects of public parochial ministry. The pastoral care and involvement with the bereaved can be significant and requires considerable patience, sympathy and sensitivity. Such cannot be learnt, although techniques concerning the pre-funeral visit and the funeral itself should be part of ministry training and formation. For the bereaved, who in the majority, although not exclusively, of situations, request a Christian minister to conduct the funeral of a departed loved one, the fact that there is a person, the parson, whose job is not only to help prepare and conduct the service, but also quite simply to care and be with those who are mourning is important and much valued. Whilst the minister will always approach the situation with professional competence and some degree of detachment which is often necessary, there will be occasions when the circumstances and nature of the death can be emotionally demanding. Such is often the case in the situation of the death of a very young person, sudden and tragic accidents, or that of a person to whom the priest was known if not close. The accessibility of the priest and Church at these most traumatic and difficult circumstances is an important if not essential part of the Church's mission and ministry within the parish. In a similar fashion to weddings, many bereaved people seek a 'designer' service which reflects something of the deceased's life and achievements. Such is in contrast the funeral service in the Book of Common Prayer which did not even provide for the mention of the deceased's name. The funeral service and related provisions in Common Worship enables and encourages a more personal approach both in the ministry towards the bereaved and in the formation of the funeral service. There are opportunities for a eulogy by family members and for the use of symbols with special resonances for the departed. These are in addition to the use of a cross (crucifix), bible (Book of the Gospels), a reading and appropriate homily.

All of this requires great sensitivity, planning and preparation. The time, however, is justified and well spent not only in meeting the needs of the bereaved but also in demonstrating the care and love of Christ through the ministry of the Church. Liturgical skills are an essential ingredient. Common Worship also provides opportunities for ministry prior to death, at death and a memorial service subsequent to the funeral. These are not always possible, given the process that many experience in respect of illness and death. The hospital setting is often the location for a final illness and the hospice for terminal situations. However, if parishioners know that their priest is always available, there will often be a request for prayers and anointing the deceased prior to removal by the local funeral director. This ministry can be especially helpful at the moment when the reality of death is directly experienced. The relationship with the local Funeral Director is often crucial in this respect, as it is for the whole of the funeral process. If they are aware that the priest is always acces-sible, they will often advise the bereaved accordingly and which can lead to ministerial opportunities shortly after death and throughout the period prior to the funeral service. Similarly, hospital chaplains will often advise parish priests of parishioners who are ill or close to death. Whilst there may be no quantifiable measure of this ministry, there can be little doubt as to how much it is appreciated. Obituaries and thank-you columns in the local newspaper often testify to this reality.

Apart from the main act of weekly worship and ongoing pastoral care, the occasional offices are the mission opportunities granted in the main to the Church of England. The Church ignores them at its peril, not because it seeks some beneficial outcome for itself, but rather because the sensitive and pastoral discharge of these responsibilities convey the truth that the Church exists for all, and especially those who are not regular attenders or supporters. It might be helpful if the Church, instead of devoting considerable time, energy and resources to new ways of encouraging people to become Christian and attend worship, it devised courses and programmes for clergy and laity as to how best to discharge their legal responsibilities to the people of the parish in exercising the rites of the occasional offices.

vi) Mission and Growth

The notion of mission (literally "being sent") is often seen as central to the Church's task. Within the tradition of the apparent words of Jesus to his disciples, 'Go therefore and make disciples of all nations, baptising them in the name of the Father and of the Son and of the Holy Spirit' (Matthew 28: 19), there is the motivation to engage in such mission, often termed 'outreach', as such proclaims the Gospel (literally 'good news') of Jesus Christ. Some would see this is in purely evangelistic terms, converting people to the Christian faith, whilst others would see it as demonstrating the love of God through service to others in a variety of ways. In any event, what mission may be in the twenty-first century is a disputed issue. What is the 'good news' of Jesus Christ, and how can such be proclaimed in a post-modern, secularist and pluralistic world, where even, as has already been identified, the onetime common grammar of God can no longer be assumed? How does the Church speak the language of God and the Gospel if there is no common language of discourse. C. Mordaunt stated this problem of mission:

> There is a gap between what the Churches do and what they feel they ought to be doing. What they actually do, mostly, is conduct

services on Sunday, visit the sick, bury the dead, run activities for children and young people and generally behave like a caring and responsible community. But when asked to state their aims they feel obliged to play down all these useful and practical things and major instead on something called "mission". What is meant by "mission" is fortunately not too closely defined, so sensible people interpret it to mean doing the above-mentioned worthwhile things in relation to non-members as well as members. But if pressed, the Church will always come down on the side of saying that it means turning non-members into members; recruiting; converting. ('Mission Difficult but not Impossible' by C Mordaunt. The Guardian, 4th June, 1994)

The necessity for recruitment, even as part of a mission strategy, often, and temptingly, outweighs all other considerations. Being the Church, not only in functional terms, is for many, attractively, what, at best, the Church is in any given community. In this sense to be the Church is representatively and historically for many the reality of the presence of God at a time when matters and issues of God are at a premium. This view lies behind Bishop Williams' defense of the parish church building. All the gimmicks available, and often experimented with by desperate clergy, do not in themselves guarantee the conversion of any individual, or the retention of those recently attracted to the Church. If the Church wishes to take seriously attracting and welcoming newcomers, it needs to look beyond the horizon of the instant, superficial and often crass expression of the Gospel that merely seeks to fill empty pews. People are not easily fooled, and the Church risks not only continued long-term decline, but also indifference, if not disparagement, by a sophisticated and educated populace. Emphasis on being a community of love, acceptance, inclusivity, tolerance and justice rather than an emporium of the latest and often untried and untested fad or whim, are perhaps more central and critical to people's perception and even need of what a Church is, as opposed to any chimera which is hardly distinguishable from many other instant-satisfaction products in the market place.

Clearly, for many within the Church, mission is linked with growth. It is not a view shared by all. One of the most interesting phenomena of religious belief and practice is the apparent affirmation of the former in the face of the neglect of the latter. It was the acknowledgement of such that inspired Grace Davie to subtitle her book, 'Religion in Britain since 1945' with 'Believing without Belonging' (1994). Richard Holloway, the former Bishop of Edinburgh and Primus of the Scottish Episcopal Church, supports this analysis:

> *What seems to be true, however, is that many people in our society, who are not necessarily hostile to faith or spirituality, see the Church as irrelevant to their own real needs and find it boring and unstimulating when they experience it. The marketing of everything in our culture has affected religion as well as everything else, and Christianity is now one brand among many in the supermarket, suffering, perhaps, from the pains of lost grandeur because once it was the only brand on sale. (R Holloway in 'Living Evangelism' ed. By Jeffrey John. London: Darton, Longman and Todd, 1996)*

Robin Gill, however, challenges the simple view that empty Churches are a result of increased secularisation:

> *If there is a single key myth that must be questioned if further analysis is to proceed, it is the following:*
>
> *"Church going decline results primarily from a gradual loss of religious belief, itself resulting from the development of scientific and rational thought in the nineteenth century, and enhanced by war and technology in the twentieth century."*
>
> *So long as this key myth remains unchallenged, the empty Church is not intellectually problematic. Occasional resurgence of Church going might still be expected among the gullible and superstitious, but amongst an increasingly educated population Church*

going would inevitably become a declining and socially insignificant
form of activity(ibid)

It is clear from current observations that mission is at the top of
the ecclesiastical agenda. Why this should be so at this particular
time is perhaps linked to what many in the Church perceive to be
a loss of faith, with the consequential decline in Church attendance. There is also the perceived threat, challenge and for many
the attack from scientific militant atheism. The desperation and
depression felt leads to both a form of protectionism and
aggression to protect existing members of the Church, and to
attract new ones. A concept of mission that entails service and
serving people where they are and what their self-defined needs
might be is lost in attempts to 'bring them in' often on the terms
already set and defined by the Church or a particular brand of
theology and ecclesiology. In a newspaper article, the Rev Dr
Joanna Collicutt McGrath draws upon the work of the distin-
guished anthropologist Mary Douglas when she points out that
sensitivities in certain Church contexts are:

> ......*particularly powerful when the viability of a small group is*
> *threatened by dominant alien cultures with which it rubs shoulders.*
> *Under these conditions shoring up group identity becomes a high*
> *priority. Boundaries become more tightly defined, and those who*
> *inhabit marginal positions become feared polluters......Conservative*
> *Anglicans feel under threat these days. So it is not surprising that*
> *they feel the need to police their boundaries with vigilance.... ('Face*
> *to Faith' by Joanna Collicutt McGrath.The Guardian, 2nd June,*
> *2007)*

Mission does not necessarily imply or require strategies to affect
Church growth. Some attempts at fresh expressions of being the
Church, or mission shaped, can often be perceived as disin-
genuous in that what they present is not what they seek. Bishop

Williams was aware of mission as being service when he wrote in the section of his book headed, 'A New Sense of Mission':

More important is the growing sense, on all sides, that the Church fellowship is not an end in itself, but is "sent" by God to live a life of service to the neighbourhood, just as the national Church is sent to serve the whole nation, and the world-Church sent to serve the whole world. (ibid)

Perhaps in order to be a truly mission-shaped church and what for many will be a fresh expression of Church, there is a need to be liberated from the obsession to increase numbers, whether of believers or of Church attenders. In one sense, it could be said that Jesus did not seek believers (in fact he was critical of those who had too much or too literal beliefs), but rather followers. It is no coincidence that the first Christians were called followers of the Way. The practice of a mission strategy of service would enhance the reputation and credibility of the Church irrespective of whether there was a consequential increase in numbers. However, combined with an effective and encouraging ministry of occasional offices, such can often result in increased support for the Church. There is a Buddhist saying that 'when the flowers begin to open, you do not have to tell the bees to come'. Mission should always be that of love and service. In the past the Church sought to meet the needs of the people, whether by the provision of free education for poorer people who otherwise would have no access to schooling, or the provision of welfare and care for the more vulnerable and disregarded. Would it not be possible for the Church to identify imaginatively areas of need within parishes that could be addressed and challenged? Growth need not be the mission priority for the Church, although there are issues concerning the continued resourcing of the Church.

There is another important way of understanding how mission can be understood and done in the twenty-first century.

Such is more about engagement with the world than seeking to convert the world or, even worse, demonise those who are outside of the community of faith. It is also about listening: hearing God speak and not necessarily within the Church. Through this process, there will come, together with others, a discernment of God's will for his/her people within the context of contemporary living, and confronting contemporary issues. 'Being sent', in this respect, is learning to attend to the presence of God in the world and to be touched and challenged by the Spirit operating within the spirit of the age. Shakespeare and Rayment-Pickard described this understanding of mission:

> *Mission can no longer be valid as a form of colonialism, patronizing or demonizing the other faiths and cultures it encounters. But the mission of God – and therefore of the Church – is something very different. It is a bearing witness in mind and heart, flesh and blood, to a commonwealth of grace ......Mission now demands that we become listeners ....To be attentive to what God is creating, where God is sending us, we need to be aware of God's presence in the world around us, and especially in the lives of those ignored or vilified by the powers that be. Making connections between the struggles and passions and dreams of our world, the missionary Church can be a bridge-builder, a community of participation and an agent for change. (ibid)*

vii) The State and Establishment

The establishment of the Church of England is not only a legal question, it is also a political one based on often unexamined theological assumptions about how the church should define its place in relation to divine order, human order (in this case, monarchy) and national territory. ('Disestablishing the Kingdom' by Tom Hurcombe in 'Setting the Church of England Free: The case for disestablishment', edited by Kenneth Leech. Croydon: The Jubilee Group, 2001)

One of the most regular and sometimes fervent criticisms leveled against the Church of England is that it is merely the 'spiritual arm' of the state. In the nineteenth century it was often classed as 'the Tory Party at prayer', although mainly by supporters of the Liberal Party! However, it is a simple matter of fact that the Church of England is by law established. Such has both a legal and formal reality, and also a practical ecclesiology. Whilst Williams perceived the advantages of having the Crown involved in senior Church appointments, he nevertheless emphasised the practical outworking of establishment in providing the Church's ministry to all within the nation, without fear or favour. Such was more appreciable in an age when there were little to no ecclesiastical or spiritual alternatives to the Church of England, and also when the Crown and Parliament were restricted to those who were Anglicans.

The Church in England became the Church of England by virtue of a series of Acts of Parliament aimed primarily, but not exclusively, to secure the divorce of King Henry VIII from his queen, Catherine of Arragon. There were a successive series of pieces of legislation which would ensure not only a separation of the Church from the authority of Rome and the Pope, but also give the King supreme control over the affairs of the Church. The main acts to secure this transfer were '*The Submission of the Clergy, 1532*':

> ...*do offer and promise, "in verbo sacerdotti", here unto your Highness, submitting ourselves most humbly to the same, that we will never from henceforth enact .... Or execute any new canons or constitutions provincial, or any other new ordinance, provincial or synodal, in our Convocation or Synod in time coming, which be, assembled only by your Highness's commandment of write, unless your Highness by your royal assent shall licence us to assemble our Convocation, and to ... execute such constitutions ...and thereto give your royal assent and authority. (Public Record Office,*

S.P.1/70, pp. 35-6)

In 1554 an Act for the Submission of the Clergy to the King's Majesty (25 Hen. VIII, c.19) gave statutory confirmation to this 1532 Submission. It was the Act of Supremacy, 1543 (26 Hen. VIII, c.1) which resolved the matter of final authority and *de facto* made the Church not only a state Church established, but very much at the beck and call of the King. The virtual unlimited powers would be exercised by Henry with little compunction or sensitivity.

> *....be it enacted by authority of this present Parliament, that the King our sovereign Lord, his heirs and successors, kings of this realm, shall be taken, accepted, and reputed the only Supreme Head in earth of the Church of England, called "Anglicana Ecclesia" and shall have and enjoy ,annexed and united to the imperial Crown of this realm, as well the title and style thereof, as all honours, dignities, pre-eminences, jurisdictions, privileges, authorities, immunities, profits, and commodities, to the said dignity of Supreme Head of the same Church belonging and appertaining.... (Stat. Realm, iii.492)*

With the exception of the brief interlude of the Catholic Queen Mary (1553-58), the title Supreme Head of the Church of England remained until the accession of the Protestant Queen Elizabeth, who in deference to sensitivities about a woman being Head, took the title Supreme Governor. This title remains to this day, and the English reformation and the establishment of the Church of England received apotheosis in the reign of Elizabeth (1558-1603), and culminated after the brief commonwealth period with the authorisation of the 1662 Book of Common Prayer This remains the standard liturgical text for the Church of England, although variations are permitted, not least in the book, Common Worship. The Prayer Book received its authority by Act of

Parliament (Act of Uniformity, which received the Royal assent on 19th May, 1662), and permissive variations were granted to the Church by Parliament, not least to avoid further parliamentary and ecclesiastical difficulties as experienced with the proposed Prayer Book revision of 1928. Colin Podmore describes the process began by Henry VIII:

> *Thus, in the reign of Henry VIII the English Church was effectively nationalized and then, to a significant extent, privatized. The king replaced the pope and seized a considerable proportion of the church's wealth, but with the notable exception of the monastic life its internal system remained intact. ('Aspects of Anglican Identity', Colin Podmore. Church House Publishing, 2005)*

Podmore describes the various changes and movements within the Church subsequent to the Henrician Reformation, but concludes by describing the position of Church and State in the twentieth century:

> *The twentieth century saw a gradual increase in the practical independence of the church from the state. In 1919 the Church Assembly, consisting of the Convocations and a House of Laity, was established to process church legislation, which Parliament would approve or reject but not amend. In 1970 a new General Synod, inheriting most of the powers of the Convocations (which continued to exist) and all those of the Church Assembly, was inaugurated. By the Worship and Doctrine Measure 1974 the General Synod received powers to authorize new and alternative services without parliamentary approval. Under a protocol of 1977 a church body, the Crown Appointments Commission (renamed the Crown Nominations Commission in 2003), was given a decisive role in the choice of diocesan bishops. (ibid.)*

However, an alternative analysis of the current situation is given by Valerie Pitt:

> *In practice, the sovereign's powers have, over the centuries, devolved to other agencies, Parliament, the Privy Council, the Prime Minister. Constitutionally the Queen does not act except on "advice". That means that the power which the Crown acquired in the sixteenth century to direct the affairs of the church is actually exercised by Parliament or by the Prime Minister. Take a "for instance": when Synod finally decided that women might be priested, its decision still had to be enacted in Parliament. And there have been occasions when Parliament has thrown out the church's proposals. Supremacy means supremacy. ('The Church by Law Established', Valerie Pitt in 'Setting the Church of England Free: The case for disestablishment', ed. Kenneth Leech. Jubilee Group, 2001)*

Whilst these changes have been beneficial for the Church, it does not change the reality that the Church of England is by law established, and that certain and final decisions relating to Church organisation and polity reside outside of ecclesiastical and synodical procedures. For many, the link with the state through the Crown, as for Bishop Williams, is an important expression of what the Church is and is seen, thereby, to be rooted in English society, as defined within a constitutional monarchy. Many, along with Bishop Williams, would value such as representing the formal belief that England is still a Christian country, that the monarch is Anglican, and that the Church of England is wedded to the fabric of the nation. However, there are obvious difficulties with the assumptions and reality of this outlook. England is not predominantly Christian but rather a nation of many faith traditions, which in terms of religious observance and practice outnumber attenders at Church of England services. Other Christian denominations have and continue to make a contribution to the English religious kaleidoscope, although the rate of decline of adherents and attenders is as sharp, if not sharper, as that for the Church of England. The institutions of the state may still reflect a Christian perspective and be served, not least through chaplaincies, by Church of England ministers, prayers may be said, assemblies in schools performed, the Archbishop of Canterbury appear at state banquets with the Queen, clergy asked for their opinion (often about things they may know little about!), but none of this alters the reality of England being a secular nation in which for the majority, the Church is of little importance of relevance.

The question must remain as to how a Church can minister to and be available to all who wish to be beneficiaries of such ministry as can be offered, without either giving gratuitous offence to other faith traditions and denominations, together with those of no faith who feel such is an imposition on the nature of a secular twenty-first century society and which, at the same time, does not compromise the essence of the gospel by close involvement with a state, which may from time to time deny gospel principles in its *modus operandi*. Clearly, the latter problematic begs the question as to what are essential gospel principles. What is not in doubt is that the Church of England still has something to offer society, and the issue is how best such can be effectuated. There is still something right about the Church of England and its position within English society whether formal, challenging or pastoral.

viii) The Church and Ethics

The call of the God experienced in Christ is simply a call to be all that each of us is – a call to offer, through the being of our humanity, the gift of God to all people by building a world in which everyone can live more fully, love more wastefully and have the courage to be all that they can be. That is how we live out the presence of God. God is about living, about loving and about being. The call of Jesus is thus not a call to be religious. It is not a call to escape life's traumas, to find security, to possess peace of mind. All of those things are invitations to a life-contracting idolatry. The call of God through Jesus is a call to be fully human, to embrace insecurity without building protective fences, to accept absence of peace of mind as a requirement of humanity. It is to see God is the experience of life, love and being who is met at the edges of an expanded humanity ('Jesus for the Non Religious', John Shelby Spong. HarperCollins:New York, 2007)

Back in the millennium year, the "Jubilee 2000" campaign for debt relief reached a climax with a huge demonstration in Birmingham in the UK, where the economic power-brokers of the G8 countries had gathered. We had brought two coach loads from my diocese in South Wales; and, as I looked at the extraordinary variety of Christian groups on the streets – Catholic, Pentecostal, outrageously left-wing and outrageously right-wing – I, like others, felt able to say, "I have seen the Church and it works." Something of a real hunger and thirst for justice in Christ's name had drawn and held this unlikely coalition; its only agenda was to further what all believed was the call of God's kingdom, to resist what offended God's justice. ('Tokens of Trust', Rowan Williams. Canterbury Press:Norwich, 2007)

It is unlikely that Bishop Williams would have used the language of Bishop Spong or Archbishop Williams to describe the outworking of ethics within the Church of England. In 1966 the Church still thought of its ethical responses to be very much at the level of the individual and matters of individual morality, especially such in respect as marriage, divorce, sex, contraception, abortion and homosexuality. In many respects, although such was not intended, the appearance of the Bishop of Woolwich, the Rt Rev Dr John Robinson, at the trial of Penguin Books and the publication of D H Lawrence's 'Lady Chatterley's Lover', reinforced this view of the Church's consideration of ethics:

He (Bishop Robinson) felt the Church's standing in society – or lack of it – very deeply. It mattered to him that the Church should speak out on certain subjects – not least the Christian understanding of sex. ('A Life of Bishop John Robinson', Eric James. Collins: London, 1987)

Eric James quotes the Archbishop of Canterbury's (Dr Geoffrey Fisher) statement to the Canterbury Diocesan Conference, 5th November, 1960:

The Bishop of Woolwich had full right to appear as a witness on the point of law involved. But to do so would obviously cause confusion in many people's minds between his individual right of judgment and the discharge of his pastoral duties. Inevitably anything he said would be regarded as said by a Bishop whose chief concern is to give pastoral advice to the people committed to his charge, and particularly in these moral questions to teachers and parents upon whom such a heavy burden of responsibility lies. (ibid)

Many recognise and affirm what is perceived to be the ethical teaching of Jesus. Many still look to the Church for ethical teaching and a response to contemporary issues, both local and national. However, it is to be noted that such calls, especially from within the national media, is of a critical nature in that Church pronouncements do not necessarily accord with some of biases of the media. Many of the dioceses of the Church of England have social responsibility departments and officers, which as well as advising the bishop and the diocese, often undertake work of a practical and ethical nature with marginal groups within society such as the disadvantaged, asylum seekers, etc.

Any systematic form of ethics, and especially such based upon a particular religion, philosophy or ideology stands to be examined and criticized. It is never self-evident that a particular ethical perspective, outlook or programme is right and applicable for all pertaining circumstances and situations. The notion of the absolute in ethical matters is at best out of touch or, at worst, tyrannical and cruel. Even from a conservative ethical position, Bishop Williams acknowledged this dimension to ethical matters and considerations.

Often the Church's response and engagement in the ethical sphere is of a challenging nature. It often does not reflect, let alone support many of what are called middle class values from what is often designated 'middle England'. There is a strong tradition within the Church of England that sees its engagement in the ethical world as representing and living Mary's Magnificat:

He has put down the mighty from their thrones, and exalted those of low degree; he has filled the hungry with good things, and the rich he has sent empty away (Luke 1: 52-53, Revised Standard Version)

The late Pope Paul VI in his encyclical *Marialis Cultus* (1974) criticised the false Mary of corrupt piety, stressing that 'Mary of Nazareth....was far from being a timidly submissive woman; on the contrary she was a woman who did not hesitate to proclaim that God vindicates the humble and oppressed, and removes the powerful people of the world from their privileged positions'.

In an article in The Times newspaper, Kenneth Leech writes of conflict within the Christian faith which has implications for any ethical position the contemporary Church may seek to adopt:

The Christian Gospel arose in the context of conflict and struggle. Galilee was the seedbed of popular revolt, and it was out of the Galilean turmoil that Jesus came with his proclamation of the Kingdom of God, of the year of jubilee, of deliverance to captives and freedom from oppression. His ministry was surrounded by conflict, his message was seen as subversive and seditious, bringing not peace but a sword, dividing families, and undermining both religious and *political establishments. The only people apparently who were reconciled by his message were Herod and Pilate…. ('Prayer: Battle for the human heart' in The Times, 25th June 1983 and quoted in 'Prayer and Prophecy: The Essential Kenneth Leech', ed. Bunch and Ritchie, DLT, London, 2009)*

Such inevitably places the Church into the political arena, a place which many Church attenders and supporters would not wish the Church to be, often seeing the Church as above politics, and being neutral in political disputes. The position is not tenable in that even a supposed neutral position is a position that can be complicit in an injustice. The realisation of human fulfillment and potential, a profoundly Christian and religious ideal, requires a just society, and one in which equality of opportunity is evidenced. Christians have to decide on which side of the fence they stand in respect of the justice and equality agenda. The teachings of Jesus leave little room for manoeuvre on this continuum.

Situation ethics, whilst running the risk of being cast adrift with every passing issue and challenge for human fulfillment, nevertheless mitigate the absolutist position of being certain from what could be an external, remote and even aloof context, failing thereby to perceive a new challenge requiring a new approach and judgment. In this respect the tradition of pastoral care as evidenced and practised by parish priests is often a better model for ethical engagement that that promulgated by hierarchies, whether such be politicians, bishops or Church synods. The radical, accepting and non-judgmental Jesus is often lost if not excluded by such.

Ecumenism

At one time in the years immediately after the Reformation, what had become the Church of England was the only Church, although there were other traditions around. Throughout its history, even when other Church traditions were able to practice their faith, the C of E has in itself witnessed to and expressed different and differing ecclesiologies; for example, the Puritans in the sixteenth and seventeenth centuries, Latitudinarians in the eighteenth century and Tractarians, Evangelicals and Catholics from the nineteenth century. A strong liberal ecclesiology within the twentieth century, together with other reforms in the Church, has been countered by the hardening of still existing traditions in the C of E. Whilst there has been significant growth within other Churches, some unified schemes both within this country and overseas, together with growing co-operation and respect, it would still be true to say that structural and institutional unity is as elusive as it ever has been. There can be little disagreement concerning the principle of Church unity, whilst at the same time respect different liturgical styles which often represent and express profound and significant differences both in theology and ecclesiology. It would also be true to affirm that in the time since Williams wrote his book, considerable progress has been made concerning respect between the Churches, and common ground in a number of often practical ways, and also in the sharing of worship. Such has been encouraging and encouraged by Council of Churches, more often now designated Churches Together, and shared activities in the form of joint collections during Christian Aid Week, and joint expressions of a common Christian commitment at times such as Holy Week and most especially during the Week of Prayer for Christian Unity in the latter part of January each year. The sharing and exchange of preachers has become a common feature of this annual event. What has not happened, except in isolated or specifically approved instances, is Eucharistic hospitality, especially between the Roman Catholic Church and the Protestant denominations, although, it should be noted, that very unofficially and without any approval, this may occur and depends in large part on the character and boldness of individual ministers.

The reality that confronts all of the so-called mainstream denominations in Britain today is that of declining congregations and increased costs, not least in terms of buildings. Those churches with full-time ministers also have the burden of paying for the same, whether from a declining and often increasingly elderly congregation, or from central church resources. The economic condition may take precedence over theological and ecclesiological sensitivities. Bishop Williams was aware of the need for greater church unity and possible integration but this was seen to be very much from a Church of England position, offering a via media between Protestantism and Catholicism as a Reformed Catholic Church. This may be the right position for the Church of England to offer to the ecumenical scene, but it may not be welcomed by all. Some form of unity without uniformity may be the preferred menu.

A Liberal Church in a Liberal Society

Over the course of the twentieth century the Christian churches in Britain declined drastically. In 1900 almost all the population had some familiarity with Christianity and about half the population attended church at least once a month. By the end of the century a majority of Britons had little or no contact with Christianity and less than 10 per cent attended church. Associated with that general pattern of decline are two important and related minor trends: the mainstream churches became increasingly liberal and church members become more selective about which of their churches' doctrines they would accept. ('Paisley: Religion and Politics in Northern Ireland', S Bruce. Oxford, 2007)

Few words are bandied about with such casual abandon as "liberal". In contemporary theological disputation, it is often assumed that everybody understands what the word means. Yet it can refer to so many different things – connected, perhaps, by family resemblance, but often by little more. ('Beware the dark side of liberalism', Giles Fraser. The Church Times, 8th May, 2009)

It does not require much perceptive observation to acknowledge that society has changed considerably over the last centuries. In particular, there have been significant changes in thought, science, knowledge and even theology since the Enlightenment of the eighteenth century, at least in that part of our planet known as the western world. In its wake, and initially in Britain, came the Industrial Revolution. This revolution, for that it is what it was, has brought many advantages to people's lives and ways of living. In particular, many of the drudgeries associated with pre-industrial work and living have been transformed, and people have been liberated from many hardships of life. The advent of the railways, motorised and aviation transportation, has shrunk not only communities, but also the globe itself, and many places previously only known through literature and the tales of travellers have become accessible to an increasing proportion of society. Advancements in medical science have rendered many previously fatal conditions obsolete, and over the past two hundred years there has been a steady increase in life spans. Whilst these changes have also brought challenges, and in some respects fragmentations of previously confined and cohesive communities, there would be few people that would wish to return to a pre-enlightenment, pre-industrial and feudal society.

This movement inevitably has consequences for Christian thought and practice. Christians live in society, unless there is a deliberate and conscious attempt to completely withdraw into isolationism, and many affirm a belief that the locus of Christianity, as an incarnational faith, is within this same and now changed society. There has, therefore, to be engagement and participation, if not accommodation. However, for many this evolution from a pre-critical understanding of faith and belief has been a tortuous one, and perceived as a conflict between faith and the new understanding. Diarmaid MacCulloch suggests that even this analysis and experience was not uniform:

> *Behind the story of European Enlightenment, which is sometimes told as a fairy-tale progression from Christian (and clerical) short-sightedness to a secularized clarity of vision, there lies a more inter-estingly complex narrative in which religion and doubt, blasphemy and devotion remained in dialogue, as they had done throughout Christian history. ('A History of Christianity', D MacCulloch, Allen Lane, 2009)*

For most of its history, the Church has made a claim to be the receiver of revealed truth. Such has been imparted through the words contained in what became defined as scripture, and thereby of significant if not the literal words from God which must be obeyed and accepted as normative and binding, not least for human behaviour, including religious practice. The evolving tradition of the Church, as its centre of gravity moved from a predominantly Jewish world to a Greek speaking and Gentile environment became important as truths were, including those of dogma and doctrine, stated through concilliar definiens of the whole Church, and the elimination of what became defined as heresy. Such was not just a religious or theological searching for revealed truth, but equally a political manoeuvre to ensure the unity of the Catholic Church within a unified Roman Empire.

The role of what became the canon of scripture has been problematic since the very beginning, when verbal stories and epistolary writings became normative and regulatory in the worship of the emerging Church. One of the problems facing the Church today, and which is open thereby to the liberal challenge of the authority of scripture, is the failure to understand the origin of scripture as scripture within the life of the embryonic Church. The rise of Christian writings to a position of scripture and authority, together with an almost equal appeal to the Hebrew scriptures, or Old or First Testament, was an unconscious process within the life of the Church. No New or Second Testament author or authors wrote as a contributor to what became the New Testament, and no biblical canon was in mind when these writings were being written, edited or read. Whatever authority, for example, apostolic or apocalyptic, was envisaged, related to the content of a particular writing, and not to a body called scripture.

In seeking to identify the liberal issue concerning the nature and supposed authority of scripture, it might be helpful to trace the authoritarian genealogy of those writings that became scripture, the Bible of the Church. The presence and inspiration of the Spirit of God (not yet as a third person of the Trinity) was and is a continuing doctrine within the Church. It is not possible to separate this belief from Christian writings. Since early

Christians regarded themselves as possessed by the same Spirit that inspired Moses and the prophets, it could be expected that their writings would come to be regarded as possessing an authority similar to that of the Old Testament, although the content of the Old Testament was not finally settled until the meeting of Rabbis at the Synod of Jamnia, about 100CE. In the early years of the Church, no other credential was required than that of inspiration for a writing to become regarded as scripture. The breadth of circulation and popularity were the remaining determinative factors in this process. On this basis, some writings, for example, First Clement and the Shepherd of Hermas, which did not fit later criteria for canonicity, attained the status of scripture in the earlier period. Hence the story of the rise of Christian writings to the status of scripture was largely that of circulation and acquaintance, not least as such were read during, and circulated, for worship. The supposed revealed truth in scripture was not only an evolving process, long after the Church came to a view that Jesus was Lord and Messiah, a view clearly not dependent upon the truths of a yet to be determined scripture, but also contingent upon circumstantial factors such as familiarity and availability.

It was with Eusebius that the process of defining a New Testament canon begins. In his 'Church History' (completed about 325CE), Eusebius itemises the early Church Fathers' opinions about Christian scriptures, together with some of his own! His listing included four gospels and the supposed letters of Paul. In dispute were James, Jude, Second Peter, Second and Third John. The Acts of Paul, the Shepherd of Hermas and Revelation were not considered genuine. Athanasius, Bishop of Alexandria, promulgated a canonical second testament list in his Easter letter of 367CE. The list is famous as it is the first to include the books to be found in the New Testament today. However, Athanasius also added a list of books to be read by those being instructed in the Christian faith, which included the

Teaching of the Apostles and the Shepherd of Hermas. There was even competition between Hebrews and the Shepherd! In the west, a Council at Hippo in 393CE enacted a second testament list comprising of the twenty seven books of the present New Testament, as did also the Synod of Carthage in 397CE.

When Judaism defined the Old Testament canon at Jamnia, a doctrine of inspiration was promulgated. No similar doctrine, however, was pronounced in the early Church when the canonical lists of Old and New Testaments were developed. The defining of a New Testament canon was not accompanied by any restriction to it of the understanding of inspiration in the Church: it was regarded as inspired, but not exclusively. The exclusion of the Shepherd of Hermas was not on the basis of inspiration, but of supposed apostolicity. There was no attempt to make the New Testament the sole writings of the Church in the west until early Calvinists appropriated the Jewish doctrine of the co-exten-siveness of inspiration with the canon. Rather, the making of the canon was a definition of a standard of inspiration, rather than a restriction or limitation of it. Thus the activity of the Spirit in the Church was not regarded as restricted to the books of the canon; rather the books of the canon defined what was of the Spirit in the Church.

It is necessary for the Church today to fully comprehend how scripture became scripture in the Church. The liberal agenda within the life of the Church is not to destroy the reality and presence of the canonical scriptures, but rather to see them as aids or resources to be drawn upon, as necessary, within worship and possible understanding of Christian belief and practice, as such has evolved through the history of the Church and Christian belief. In many respects, scripture cannot be regarded as normative or determinative for Church practice, let alone that of moral values and ways of living. There may be helpful insights, but writings from many centuries previous cannot speak author-itative to contemporary issues and decision making without evaluation and interpretation. The appeal to 'the Bible says' is not an intelligent or reasonable way to address complex modern issues. Marcus J Borg summarises the situation:

> But if the Bible's authority is not to be grounded in its origin in God, why then does it have authority for Christians? The answer is that our spiritual ancestors declared these documents to be authoritative, to be sacred scripture .... (T)his way of seeing the Bible's origin and authority goes with the historical-metaphorical interpretation of the Bible.... (W)e best understand the Bible when we set its texts in their ancient contexts and when we are attentive to their metaphorical meanings as well – that is, their more-than-literal, more-than-factual, more-than-historical meanings. (ibid.)

Issues of significant societal changes in moral matters and challenges arose in the post second world war period and has impacted upon the Churchs' response. Major legislative changes in the 1960s concerning capital punishment, abortion and homosexuality, together with a more liberated approach to life amongst young people, confronted the Church with the challenge of acceptance, accommodation or rejection of the public change of mood and opinion in all of these areas. Other issues concerned the relaxation of rules and proscriptions in respect of theatre, cinema and television productions and performances. The changing role of women in society and the availability of the contraceptive pill and the increased likelihood of pre-marital sex presented Church leaders with the dilemma of whether to resist liberal progress or to retreat to a position of condemnation and consolidation about matters which the Bible has little to nothing to say, and clearly cannot speak with any integrity or authority to the contemporary situation. The late Nigel Yates writes:

> It is also important to emphasize that, although many of the Christian

leaders in Britain supported all or some of these reforming measures, there was a solid phalanx in most of the churches that felt that their leaders had betrayed them and rejected essential Christian doctrines in their willingness to make religion more relevant to contemporary society. ('Love Now, Pay Later?' N. Yates, SPCK, 2010)

Adrian Thatcher, however, affirms that:

(T)he pre-eminence of the literal sense of the understanding of scripture in the minds of readers has eclipsed other possibilities of meaning ......the liberal tradition of theological thought can, and should, claim to be central to the older Tradition of the Church .....Tradition is too important to be left to so-called traditionalists who actually impose their own patriarchal values on the Tradition and then have the rest of the Church believe their version of it alone is true and authentic. ('Reading the Bible Today', A. Thatcher, Opening address at the Modern Church Conference, July, 2011).

A truly Liberal Church will recognise and affirm the need to allow new insights and truths to challenge previously received ideas, even if such come from supposed authoritative traditions, including biblical and ecclesiastical statements. George Newlands suggests that:

Citation of authority is never enough. The wisdom of the past may simply have been rendered obsolete – though oddly enough, theologians who ignore much of the past two hundred years of academic scholarship are often those who stress most vigorously the importance of tradition. It seems that authentic tradition stops with Aquinas, or at least, with Calvin. It is as though the Holy Spirit took early retirement around 1300 AD, and certainly would never be associated with any thought which might have been influenced by the proton pseudo of all modern thought, Immanuel Kant. ('Humane Spirit: Towards a Liberal Theology of Resistance and Respect',

George M. Newlands in 'Religious Pluralism and the Modern World: An Ongoing Engagement with John Hick' ed. Sharada Sugirtharajah. Basingstoke: Palgrave Macmillan, 2012).

The Church of England has always acknowledged its own inclusive position in society. In his 'Laws of Ecclesiastical Polity', Richard Hooker, writing in the sixteenth century, sought to affirm this inclusivity as a via media between the rival positions of a recusant Catholicism and a strident Puritanism. This is the Anglican inheritance which persisted, even after the hiatus of the Commonwealth period under Oliver Cromwell, when the Church of England went underground, and up to the very recent past when differences in theology, ecclesiology, liturgical expression and moral issues around sexuality threaten not only the inclusivity and cohesion of the Church, but even its sustainability as a recognisable ecclesiastical identity. In his most recent book, Richard Holloway, a former Bishop of Edinburgh and Primus of the Scottish Episcopal Church, writes concerning the muddles of human existence:

Unfortunately, there are no magical deliverers who can deliver us from ourselves and our muddles. No infallible Bible. No infallible Church, No infallible anything. And there never has been. Nevertheless, I find it hard to deny others the consolation of believing they have found one that works for them. Anglicanism had never claimed that kind of infallibility for itself. It knew it was a muddle; a muddled Church for muddled people. And since there were lots of muddled people around, it had an honourable vocation. ('Leaving Alexandria: A Memoir of Faith and Doubt', Richard Holloway. Edinburgh: Canongate Books, 2012)

A Liberal Church is an open and inclusive Church which respects the views of the many, and often differing theological and ecclesiological perspectives. It is not self-assertive, but humble in the light of new and fresh insights from a variety of disciplines and sources. A Church that does not open itself, even to the point of exposure and vulnerability, to truths not previously acknowledged or experienced is not faithful to the incarnation of God within the human condition. Furthermore, a Church that merely or constantly relies upon even so-called foundational texts of previous ages without challenge or question, risks further alienation and marginalisation. It does little justice to the God who is passionate about the human predicament, and as made known and exemplified in the life of Jesus. A Liberal Church will not discard these texts and documents, but, rather, will continuously seek to interpret and apply them to the contemporary situation and context, and in the light and reality of twenty-first century knowledge and experience. Such a Church is necessary for the future, both in terms of its own survival, but also in the challenges it can bring to contemporary society. It is also a Church which will affirm the importance of doubt within the context of a faith that addresses and speaks to the twenty-first century. Holloway suggests that:

> (T)he word faith is the giveaway. The opposite of faith is not doubt, it is certainty. Where you have certainty, you don't need faith. (ibid.)

A former Bishop of Lincoln, John Saxbee, posed the relevant question:

> Openness, honesty, creative listening, hearing and responding in a world of cultural and religious diversity – if these altogether innocuous and quite unexceptional qualities constitute liberalism, then what has all the fuss been about?('Liberal Evangelism: a Flexible Response to the Decade', John Saxbee. London: SPCK, 1994)

What indeed?

Ministry for Today

The Church of England is agonizing over the issue of maintaining the ordained ministry at a level and strength that is commensurate with being the Church of the nation, ministering, in theory at least, to all, whilst at the same time satisfying vociferous demands from countless parishes for their own parson. There are two primary constraints to securing these objectives: numbers and finance. Both are at a premium at the present time. There is the need, therefore, for the Church of England, to engage a fresh appraisal of the nature, form and deployment of its clergy, and as matter of some urgency. Whilst it is important to appraise the contemporary context within which ministry functions, with a view to determining what is feasible, possible and desirable, it is equally important to determine core principles and functions of the Church, and for which ministry is the delivering component.

Even a new edifice has to have foundations. For a Church considering the nature and form of ministry, there is the need to build upon what has been given in terms of the orders of the Church, with forms and structures that serve the needs of the present. In marketing terms such is the determination of the core purpose, and the necessary structures and staff to serve the same. This is particularly the case for the Church of England with a practical ecclesiology different to that of many other Churches. An appropriate, relevant and practical ecclesiology must consider the necessary essential features of, and for the Church to be the Church, in any given situation or community. The late Dutch Dominican theologian, Edward Schillebeeckx suggests:

> ...that as far as the New Testament is concerned the community has
> a right to a minister or ministers and to the celebration of the

Eucharist. ('Ministry: a case for change', SCM Press, 1981)

He continues to assert that this:

> ....*apostolic right has priority over the church order which has in fact grown up and which in other circumstances may have been useful and healthy. (ibid)*

Because Schillebeeckx' thinking on this issue is relevant for the Church today, it is worth further thought in respect of the relationship between the Christian community and the Eucharist. He writes:

> *The ancient church and the modern church cannot envisage any Christian community without the celebration of the eucharist. There is an essential link between local ecclesia and eucharist. Throughout the pre-Nicene church it was held, evidently on the basis of Jewish models, that a community in which at least twelve fathers of families were assembled had the right to a priest or community leader and thus to the eucharist, at which he presided. In the small communities, these originally episcopal leaders soon became presbyteral leaders, pastors. In any case, according to views of the ancient church a shortage of priests was an ecclesiastical impossibility. The modern so-called shortage of priests therefore stands to be criticized in the light of the ancient church's view of church and ministry, because the modern shortage in fact has causes which stem from outside the ministry, namely the conditions with which the ministry has already been associated a priori, on not specifically ecclesiological grounds. (ibid)*

A primary concern, therefore, for the modern Church should be the ensuring of the Eucharist within every Christian community, and thereby enable the authorisation, accreditation or ordination of those with appropriate gifts to fulfill the desired and necessary ministerial task and tasks. Andrew Davison and Alison Milbank in emphasising the importance of the Eucharist as central to the life and witness of the parish write:

> The parish through its whole life is empowered by liturgical praxis, and by the synergy between the Holy Spirit and the Christian body, which catches it up into the Divine life....We have argued that the parish as a mixed community is the appropriate site of reconciliation, where different sorts of people may learn to live together peaceably and with forgiveness. This is effected primarily through our Eucharistic life together. ('For the Parish: A Critique of Fresh Expressions', Andrew Davison and Alison Milbank. London: SCM Press, 2010)

As far as the Church of England is concerned the celebration, significance and importance of the Eucharist as a, if not the core activity, is bound up with the ministry of priests or presbyters, and has to be given due recognition in any attempt or process of change. Kenneth Mason confirms this necessity when he writes concerning the early and embryonic Church:

> How did Christians perceive their own Christian belonging? The answer has to include a bold reference to the Eucharist as the very heart of church life at that time. Whatever individual Christians might do, laymen, presbyters or bishops, the church as a whole knew that the Eucharistic liturgy was its most characteristic activity. It was for this that God had called it into being; it was upon this that its existence depended. ('Priesthood and Society', Kenneth Mason, Norwich: Canterbury Press, 1992)

Implicit within this objective could be the relinquishing of the traditional concept of the English vicar or parson, as the one who is expected to know everything and to do everything. The need to respect and acknowledge different ministerial skills is important for re-defining and re-constructing the functioning of both the ordained and lay ministry. Ministers, working collectively and co-operatively, are essential, not only in terms of utilising differing skills and abilities, but also in ensuring a fulfilling and rewarding exercise of Christian ministry. However, it is also essential that the Church utilises the gift it has already received and exercised over the past two millennia, namely the three fold ministry of bishop, priest and deacon. The latter is sadly wasted in the majority practice of the Church of England, where there is little understanding of the value and potential importance of a distinctive diaconate as exercised, for example, in the Church of Sweden. To use the ministry of deacons solely as a year-long probationary period, prior to priesting, undermines both the ministry of priest and deacon. The diaconate could incorporate many of the other types of ministry now being considered and implemented by the Church. Such would have two beneficial outcomes: firstly, it would demonstrate to communities that the diversity of Anglican ministry is both recognised and incorporated into the historic orders of the Church - even the title reverend and a clerical collar would make an important statement about the significance of ministry, and any minister in the Church for communities; secondly, it would encourage more vocations to the Church's ministry at a time when such appears to be at a premium. It is also important within this debate to affirm that the suggestion of the priority of the Eucharist for Church life and ministerial practice is not to undermine or displace other worship expressions, or even to suggest that the ministry of priests trump all other ministerial manifestations; it is an attempt to suggest that the gathering of the faithful around the table of the Lord and being fed with his sacramental body and blood, in loving remembrance following the Last Supper command, is an essential part of what the Church is and how the servants of the Church, the ministers represent and perform this reality and function. Daniel Hardy expressed the importance of the Eucharistic celebration as:

> ......*a drama involving God as well as us, the history of God's right-
> eousness in the world in Jesus Christ as well as its actuality for us
> by the Holy Spirit in our particular situations. In that way, it
> provides the <u>active conditions for our righteousness,</u> and serves as
> the basis for social life in the world.* ('Finding the Church', Daniel
> W Hardy. London: SCM Press, 2001)

Furthermore, in order to avoid accusations of priestcraft or
Mass-saying priests, it should be noted that in the early Church
the celebration of the Eucharist was always linked with pastoral
engagement and practice. Even those who may advocate lay
presidency at the Eucharist would assert the need for appropriate accreditation and possible calling; such is the nature of
ordination, with the added ingredient of universal approval and
appointment through the bishop. Bishop Williams affirmed the
importance of the Parish Communion as a welcome development
of Church life in the 1960s; the same is true for the Church of
England today.

There can be little doubt about what some might call a crisis
in ministry at the level of vocations, cost and ambivalence of role.
As Schillebeeckx suggested in respect of the supposed shortage
of priests, much actually comes from outside of a theology or
ecclesiology of Christian ministry, both in history and the
present. Much of the anxiety is simply self-induced, and can be
easily rectified in terms of a more relaxed and imaginative
approach to both selection and training. Perhaps Michael
Ramsey was more right than what some might give him credit
for today when he identified four aspects of priesthood: priest as
teacher and preacher, priest as minister of reconciliation, priest
as a person of prayer, and priest as person of the Eucharist. He
writes:

Man of theology, man of reconciliation, man of prayer, man of the Eucharist; displaying, enabling, involving the life of the Church – such is the ordained priest....Yet it is far from true that while the Church is our Lord's creation the ministry is only a device whereby the Church can be effective. Both Church and ministry are gifts of the divine Lord Jesus. ('The Christian Priest Today', Michael Ramsey. London: SPCK, 1972)

In any consideration as to appropriate ministerial forms for the Church of today, due regard must be given to the people the Church is called to serve, whilst at the same time acknowledging and working with the given and present structures and discipline of the Church in terms of the appropriate and authorised functioning of ministers. This does not preclude, limit or restrict necessary developments which are desirable for a Church ministering in different and rapidly changing situations. But it does mean that we build upon what we have been given, and be ever mindful of those outside of ecclesiastical structures, who may not be so imaginative and bold as those who inhabit the corridors of Church power and decision making.

To ensure that the Church of England is still right for the present generation, more priests (presbyters) are required. A more imaginative use of non-stipendiary or locally-ordained ministers, together with a positive affirmation of the ministry of the retired could assist in the growth and development of the Church's ministry. This would be in stark opposition to what appears more like a government deficit reduction or a Greek austerity approach to a reduction in numbers. A Church in retreat is unlikely to commend itself to the communities of the nation and to individual needs represented in the people of the parishes. It is also important to link such a development with a practical appraisal and use of a distinctive diaconate which could incorporate a variety of ministerial practices and needs in the parishes. To ordain more ministers is not only a possibility, but also a necessity for the Church of England. The presence of a 'vicar' in every parish would be more important, recognised and accepted by and within communities than the invention of new and uninspiring titles as 'pioneer' or 'focal' ministers. Such may be understood within the inner ecclesiastical circles whose covens invent them, but little understood and accepted beyond the same.

Marketing

Marketing is not the art of finding clever ways to dispose of what you make. Marketing is the art of creating genuine customer value. It is the art of helping your customers become better off. The marketer's watchwords are quality, service, and value. ('Marketing Insights from A to Z', Philip Kotler. Wiley & Sons: New Jersey, 2003)

......all organizations necessarily have links with the outside world; such links are the stuff of marketing. The government department which wishes to influence motorists not to drink and drive will use market research to discover the motivations of those who do, and the most effective means of influencing them......even the smallest charity has to decide who its clients are, and what are their needs, before communicating with them. ('Marketing', David Mercer. Blackwell: Oxford, 1992)

The failure to discern a market for the Church to operate within, implies an inability to perceive market segments, and consequential market targets, together with ambiguity concerning a marketable product. These are essential ingredients for the marketing recipe, but how can such relate to what the Church describes as its role and mission in contemporary society? Can the Church of England discern a marketing strategy that addresses both its core activity and the needs of its consumers, both actual and potential. Stevens and Loudon suggest that:

Churches and ministries face a number of problems which would be treated as marketing problems if they were found in the business sector. Churches and ministries are having difficulty attracting and maintaining active members/supporters; they are having difficulty determining if they are meeting these peoples' needs; and they are unable to explain why members and supporters leave or stop supporting their organizations. In many instances they suffer from poor images or just a lack of knowledge about how to effectively communicate what their organization is and the ways in which it could serve people. There are not many churches or ministries that don't have some problems that stem from their relationships with their constituents. ('Marketing for Churches and Ministers', R E Stevens and D L Loudon. Haworth Press: New York, 1992)

There are many tensions within the contemporary Church of England, not least as it seeks both survival and growth. It has also to confront the issue of needing customers from within a market where there are increasing choices and competition for people's time, commitment, engagement and resources. The implications of considering marketing as a relevant and applicable tool have more far-reaching considerations than just the discipline itself, but raise issues concerning the nature of the Church, as a twenty-first century institution seeking to attract customers as members of congregations.

The problem facing the Church and parochial clergy, who carry much of the responsibility for Church maintenance and mission, is one of significant decline in congregations, coupled with a significant increase in costs for ministry and buildings. Any medium-size business would recognise the longer-term implications of this situation. Michael Hinton describes the dilemma for the clergy:

If they excel in anything, it is usually pastoral care. They are as conscientious and respectable as they have ever been. They tend to individualism, but less than formerly to eccentricity. By the public at large they are regarded with amused indifference, tinged in the case of people who have actually come across them with regard. Their congregations, though less deferential than in the past, are usually content to accept their leadership, to tolerate their inadequacies, and to treat them affectionately. They stand in need of such kindness, since they are confronted with a host of intractable problems: the relentless advance of secularism, the financial and administrative burdens connected with one or several parishes, the requirement to balance the needs of their congregations against those of the wider community, the inadequacy of resources, the lack of time. (ibid.).

In terms of adopting some form of marketing technique or practice for the Church, the key component for delivery would be the clergy, supported and encouraged by senior colleagues and diocesan training and programmes. There is little evidence that such exist, let alone understood. However, an ostrich type approach to a major discipline such as marketing, which functions throughout society in delivering new customers and retaining old ones is clearly an effective and productive device that cannot be ignored by the Church. At this point, it is perhaps worth observing and acknowledging three fundamental principles: there is still a considerable degree of faith and faith interest in the market, even if such does not translate into religious practice. Secondly, the Church will never flourish unless and until it recognises competing products, both in terms of spirituality and social opportunities, and with which it will need to co-operate and possibly compete. Thirdly, the discipline of marketing is not principally, primarily or essentially about selling; it is about researching and determining needs, addressing and meeting them. Such is not always as it might seem. For example the managing director of a cosmetics manufacturing company once opined that in the factory it made cosmetics, in the shop it sold hope! Another example concerning the confusion between what is sold and what is sought is the customer who purchases a quarter inch drill but in fact does not really want the drill, but rather a quarter inch hole. The drill is merely the purchased tool to secure the desired end product. The difficulty for the Church, often expressed by clergy who are ambivalent or hostile towards marketing as a mission tool, concerns the product that the Church offers. At one level, it is simply the being of God with supposedly consequential benefits which may take a variety of forms depending upon one's theology. An interesting observation made by Marcus J Borg concerns the idea and experience of salvation. Borg challenges the notion that Christianity is about an afterlife and that salvation not about securing an afterlife, begging the question as to what is the Church's product. He writes:

> My answer ......is that our product is <u>salvation as the twofold transformation of ourselves and the world.</u> ('ibid.').

There will be other definitions and many will have a theological pedigree and appropriateness, but the question remains as to what the Church is really offering to people in the twenty-first century? If the Church is unsure, then its customers will be unsure as to what is on offer and whether it is for them.

The marketing dilemma for the Church has been expressed by Richard Holloway:

> What seems to be true, however, is that many people in our society, who are not necessarily hostile to faith or spirituality, see the Church as irrelevant to their own real needs and find it boring and unstimulating when they experience it. The marketing of every-thing in our culture has affected religion as well as everything else, and Christianity is now one brand among many in the supermarket, suffering, perhaps, from the pains of lost grandeur because once it was the only brand on sale. (Introduction, Richard Holloway in 'Living Evangelism', ed. Jeffrey John. London: Darton, Longman and Todd, 1996).

Marketing offers the Church a potential methodology for promoting both the Church as an institution, but also God and spirituality in its various forms and manifestations. A consequential brand loyalty to the local Church, which already exists in many places, with possible increased subscriptions, would enable not only institutional survival but also forms of growth which may not be directly connected with significant and increased Sunday Church attendance. Good market research, within local communities and congregations, would enable not only the identification of what customers and potential customers already value or expect from the Church, but also what other and additional services could legitimately be provided by the local Parish Church.

One of the main areas any marketer must address in seeking to commend the Church to customers or in determining customer desire, concerns existing ambivalence or even prejudice towards the Church. An introverted Church with little to commend itself in terms of community engagement, will be difficult to 'sell' in a potentially negative environment. The key to any marketing strategy or programme is to convey the positive fact that the Church exists and functions for those who are not necessarily part of the regular congregation or supporters. There is then the consequential need to ascertain what potential customers or supporters might want from their Parish Church. For many Churches and diocesan programmes, such necessitates a paradigmatic shift from seeking the views and wishes of those already within the life of the Church, to researching those outside. This is not to ignore existing customers, but rather to point out the obvious that new customers may have differing needs and wants than those who are already part of the life of the Church. Theodore Levitt asserted:

> ......*early decline and certain death are the fate of companies whose policies are geared totally and obsessively to their own convenience at the total expense of the customer. (ibid.)*

Amen to that!

A Contemporary Parochial Ecclesiology

The parish church has always been a complex pottage of competing convictions and interests, brought together in the focus of a building and a ministry, the ownership of which has always been open to interpretation. What the parish church needs now, arguably, is to continually rediscover its ministry, one that engages with culture in creative ways. ('Many rooms in my Father's house: The changing identity of the English Parish Church', Martyn Percy in 'The Future of the Parish System', ed. Steven Croft. London: Church House Publishing, 2006).

In the local press, the Church's role in community life – providing care, taking responsibility, focusing local activities, and all the rest of it – is described and acknowledged. In this context, there is nothing <u>odd</u> about the place of the Church. It is almost never portrayed as a form of peculiar interest group. Quite the contrary, it is an intrinsic part of the local scene, and one of the main points of reference for people in a particular place. ('The Anglican Church as a Polity of Presence', Ben Quash in 'Anglicanism: The Answer to Modernity', ed. Duncan Dormor, Jack McDonald and Jeremy Caddick. London: Continuum, 2003).

There is still something right about a parish church serving a local community, and representing the presence of God. For many churches and parishes, this has been the case for centuries. More modern churches on new estates, and in new towns perform and fulfill the same function of being and serving. The critical issue is how relevant, appropriate and necessary is such in the twenty-first century, when even the rumour of God seems muted, if not silent, and the practice of worship in the parish church has long ceased to be a priority or experience in the lives of the majority? In what sense, therefore, can we speak of a contemporary ecclesiology, and how would this work in a positive and sustainable way in the parishes of our nation?

There are a number of current and critical factors which could be observed, and whilst there will be some obvious exceptions, the general principle holds:

1   The Parish Church is a recognisable brand, even if not fully understood or purchased;

2   The Vicar or Rector, perhaps even acknowledged as the Parish Priest, is a recognisable person within the community. He or she may be misunderstood, sometimes ridiculed, but the designation figures alongside that of the local doctor, councillor, police officer or other functionary within the parish;

3   There is still a residual understanding that people go to Church to worship. This may not be something that is accessed or participated in by the majority, but many know this is what happens on a Sunday. There is more likely to be contact through the occasional offices of baptism, marriage or funeral services;

4   Christmas is still a major attraction for parishioners, and many will attend some form of carol service or put in an appearance at the Midnight Mass. This is embedded in the culture of most parishes. Such may extend to Easter, Remembrance Sunday and a Harvest Festival, although the latter is losing its inculturation, as many do not have any direct or experiential contact with the land or farming.

The aforementioned are given and can be readily witnessed in the life of many parishes. It is puzzling, therefore, that many within the Church fail to appreciate these realities, not least as something that can be built upon. The merging or even elimination of parishes, designated by little understood titles, and the creation of more and enlarged multi-parish benefices simply removes the local Church away from the direct experience of the local community. Bishop Williams acknowledged this issue in 1966. The brand and loyalty to the local Church is thereby significantly weakened and possibly eroded. Similarly, creating new ministerial titles and designations only exist to confuse those familiar with existing forms. If few understand what the title refers to, it is unlikely that the minister will be acknowledged, appreciated or even used. It was not so long ago that the Royal Mail changed its title to Consignia, and very quickly had to revert. This ought to be a warning to those who think that changing a few titles here or there, and re-structuring a familiar and easily understood system will enable the Church to reach out to and attract those who have had little to no contact with the Church over many years, or even at all.

A contemporary parochial ecclesiology, therefore, needs to evidence two fundamental principles: firstly, begin where you are, and build upon what is already understood and possibly valued; secondly, instead of researching or talking to existing churchgoers, seek those who rarely attend Church for their views and opinions about the existence of the parish church and parochial ministers. Many dioceses have been undertaking a review of ministerial deployment, given what is perceived to be a reduction in vocations to the ordained ministry and difficulty in resourcing the full-time stipendiary ministry. However, such has been done almost solely within the Church, often at deanery and parochial levels. It is not difficult to observe lay representatives seeking to preserve and retain their own minister, although there are some honourable exceptions. The approach is not only flawed at a number of significant levels, including an inability to effect research in a statistically valid manner, but also in its limited and myopic framework. The Church and the parishioners of any given parish deserve much more than this.

A further ecclesiological confusion exists and is even promoted in the practice of many churches. This is the designation of church attenders as members. It is a profoundly un-Anglican description, and creates a self-limiting factor for those who are thereby not members. There is no such thing as a member of the Church of England; the defining category is that of parishioner. Membership of the Catholic Church, of which the Church of England is a professed part, is given at baptism, and the only other thing an Anglican can be a member of is the Church Electoral Roll, for the sole purpose of electing and standing for office within the Church. Other Churches have members; the Church of England does not. Whilst the confusion may be understandable, it is unhelpful in defining and exercising parochial ministry and pastoral care. The Parish Priest is not chaplain to congregation, but rather a priest and pastor to the whole community. This reality is given tangible effect through the election of Churchwardens by the whole parish, and the right of all parishioners to access the ministry of the Church as a right. The Church ignores this at its peril, and fails to discern the Gospel proclamation and living on a much wider canvas than that of those who regularly attend the worship of the Parish Church. This is not to suggest that these people should be ignored or disregarded, but rather to affirm their equality with the parishioners of the parish.

What, therefore, should the contemporary Church look like? In many respects, not least given what has already been argued, not much different to what it has been in the past, reflecting practices that Bishop Williams upheld back in 1966. The physical presence of a recognisable and observable parish church is an essential ingredient on the ecclesiological matrix. It could be observed that the church building is sacramental in that it is an outward and visible presence of an inward and spiritual grace. However, our parish churches should be places for the community, and not just for those of the community who gather for worship. In many respects, the parish church should revert to what it was in medieval times, a place of gathering for the people to undertake and engage in community functions. This was made difficult or impossible by the introduction of fixed pieces of furniture into the nave, thereby restricting the use, primarily in the form of pews, for worship only. A good principle would be that of returning the parish church to the people of the parish. This would not exclude, limit or restrict the use of the building for the primary purpose of worship; it would merely open up a holy place to more people for a variety of events and functions. A wider community focus would thereby be the added value of the parish church. More modern churches usually possess this flexibility of use and space, and use the same to good and positive effect. The challenge would be to facilitate the same in medieval buildings, bedeviled with Victorian furniture. A core group of people assembled by the Grubb Institute wrote in a piece sub-titled 'The local church in its community':

Some churches will be barely conscious of their local community, neither will the community take much notice of the church. For example, the members assemble and disperse without any fuss and the ministers make little attempt to visit those who are not church attenders. Other churches, however, have an influence upon the community such that members of that community begin to consider the church as "theirs", without any conscious decision to attend it or to make obvious use of it under normal circumstances. The church building and the fact of its presence provide a religious focus for them; and in times of need, relating to birth, marriage, illness and death, men and women who have hitherto shown no link with the church make demands on its ministers. ('The Parish Church?' ed. Giles Ecclestone. London & Oxford: Mowbray, 1988)

The role, purpose and function of the parish priest and other ministers are also important aspects of a contemporary ecclesi-ology. Significant questions have to be raised about many of the assumptions behind much of what the parish priest is expected to do. Chairing a multiplicity of Church meetings, and being involved with a plethora of Church groups may not be the best use of his/her time and energies. Attention to the needs of the community within which the Church is located and putting the time and energy of the Church to the task of serving the community is not only likely to be more productive in terms of the Church's witness and possible support, but also is a Gospel principle that trumps most other manifestations of ecclesial life. The marketing principle and imperative of looking out of the window rather than looking into the mirror has theological and Christological validity and represents a necessary and contem-porary ecclesiological methodology. Our churches need to change, but not too much!

Conclusion

This book has attempted to reflect upon the thoughts of a previous Bishop of Leicester, Ronald Williams, in his book 'What's Right with the Church of England'. It has sought to demonstrate how the issues of 1966 are not significantly different to the issues facing the Church of England in 2012. However, there is also the belief and affirmation that what Williams portrayed as being right with the Church of England some 46 years ago is still right for the Church at the present time. Quite simply this is representing the reality and presence of God within every community, facilitating the worship of God in Christ in every parish, and effecting pastoral care, concern and challenge. The continued offering of baptism, marriage and funerals is demonstrably an important part of the service that the Church offers, and it is clearly valued as something that many seek, even if such does not translate into regular worship or support. In an age that in many respects and somewhat pejoratively is described as 'secular', it is of interest that many still value the Church and would wish to call upon its ministry. Alan Billings' description of cultural Christians is significant. However, the Church needs to avoid overt and aggressive evangelistic programmes in order to secure converts and growth. Even if opinions are not already formed about church techniques, they soon would be, and any understanding or appreciation of the Church as servant to the community would quickly evaporate. The desperation of many churches and clergy to either grow numbers attending and supporting the Church, or at the least stem any haemorrhage of decline can easily be counter-productive. Churches will grow when they are perceived and experienced as having relevance and significance within the life of the parish, confronting and addressing both individual and corporate need and issues.

The matter not specifically addressed by Williams and this book, concerns the current issue of human sexuality, paranoia within certain sections of the Church about gay marriage, ordination and women is a diverting and destructive aspect of church perception within wider society. Although Bishop Williams did not perceive the future intensity and even aggressiveness of the current debate and debacle, as a former theological college principal, he could not have been unaware of the number of ordinands and priests who were gay. At a time when such was not admitted, and the 'don't ask, don't tell' rubric was applied, there was little controversy. The same cannot be said of 2012! It is a good thing that clergy are open and honest about themselves, including their sexuality and partnerships. It has to be acknowledged, although rarely such, given the ferocity of the debate, that issues of sex and sexuality are not a core Gospel or biblical issue. Very little is to be found in the Bible about these matters; the pathological obsession about gender and sex is to be located more in the fantasies of those who take a negative and hostile view of gay people and women. There is more in the Bible and the teaching of Jesus about wealth and justice, and which, ironically, are not given prominence within the life and witness of the wider church. This would indicate a level of disturbance and dissonance that can only indicate a very unhealthy mindset on the part of those promoting the current debate, and a serious failure to engage the more fundamental principles of the Gospel. It is to be hoped that the Church, and those with warped ideas and fantasies, will grow up and grow out of the present obsessions in a similar way to which the Church in the past has grown up and grown out of other supposedly significant issues. If the Church of England, unlike some other branches of the Anglican Communion, and in solidarity with more liberal and progressive representations of the Christian faith, can stand alongside all marginal and maligned groups within the society, it will be performing a vital ecclesiological function that will demonstrate that there is still something right about the Church of England.

Williams was right about the rightness of the Church of England in 1966. The Church of England can still be right for the people of this nation and beyond in 2012.

Bibliography

WILLIAMS, R.R. (1966), *What's Right with the Church of England.* London: Lutterworth Press

SANDBROOK, D. (2006), *White Heat: a History of Britain in the Swinging Sixties.* London: Little Brown

MOORE, S. (10ᵗʰ April, 1993), 'Ad Gloriam', *Guardian Weekend*

PERCY, M. (2010), *Shaping the Church: the Promise of Implicit Theology.* London: Ashgate

MOLTMAN, J. (1980), 'Christianity and the World Religions' in HICK, J. and HEBBLETHWAITE, ed. *Christianity and Other Religions.* London: Fount

JONES, C., a future Pentecostal minister arriving in Britain, 1955, quoted in KYNESTON, D. (2009), *Family Britain.* London: Bloomsbury Publishing

DAWKINS, R. (2006), *The God Delusion.* London: Bantam Press

Working as One Body, 1995: the Report of the Archbishops' Commission on the Organisation of the Church of England. London: Church House Publishing

GILL, R. (1993), *The Myth of the Empty Church.* London: SPCK

HINTON, M. (1994), *The Anglican Parochial Clergy: a Celebration.* London: SCM Press

LEVITT, T. (1986), *The Marketing Imagination.* New York: The Free Press

ROBERTS, R. (1991), *Letter to the Independent*

FRASER, G. (2007), *Christianity with Attitude.* Norwich: Canterbury Press

KEIGHTLEY, A. (1976), *Wittgenstein, Grammar and God.* London: Epworth Press

BORG, M.J. (2011), *Speaking Christian: Recovering the lost meaning of Christian words.* London: SPCK

KYNASTON, D. (2007), *Austerity Britain 1945-1951.* London: Bloomsbury Press

DAVIE. G. (1994), *Religion in Britain since 1945.* London: Blackwell

BILLINGS, A. (2004), *Secular Lives, Sacred Hearts.* London: SPCK

JOHN, J. (ED) (1996), *Living Evangelism.* London: Darton, Longman and Todd

McFAGUE, S. (1987), *Models of God.* London: SCM Press

AMBROSE, A. (ED) (1979), *Wittgenstein's Lectures Cambridge 1932-1935.* Oxford

KERR, F. (1986), *Theology after Wittgenstein.* Oxford: Blackwell

BIERCE, A. (1967), *The Enlarged Devil's Dictionary.* London: Victor Gollancz

DOSTOYEVSKY, F. (1958), *The Brothers Karamazov, Volume 1.* Middlesex: Penguin Books

DAVIES, P. (2006), *The Goldilocks Enigma.* London: Penguin Books

PHILLIPS, D. Z. (2004), *The Problem of Evil and the Problem of God.* London: SCM Press

MOLTMAN, J. (1974), *The Crucified God.* London: SCM Press

WIESEL, E. (1972), *Night.* London: Fontana Books

HEDGES, C. (2007), *New Statesman,* 4th June

SHAKESPEARE, S. and RAYMENT-PICKARD, H. (2006), *The Inclusive God: Reclaiming Theology for an Inclusive Church.* Norwich: Canterbury Press

HOLLOWAY, R. (2012), *Review of The Face of God, the Gifford Lectures by Roger Scruton.* New Statesman, 2nd April

PERHAM, M. (ED) (1991), *Liturgy for a New Century.* London: SPCK

STEVENSON, K. and SPINKS, B. (1991), *The Identity of Anglican Worship.* London: Mowbray

LAWRENCE, D.H. (1969), *Apropos of Lady Chatterley's Lover.* London: Heinemann

STEVENSON, K. (1989), *The First Rites.* London: Lamp Press

ECCLESTONE, G. (ED) (1988), *The Parish Church.* Oxford: Mowbray

MORDAUNT, C. (1994), *Mission Difficult but not Impossible.* The

Guardian, 4th June

McGRATH, J.C. (2007), *Face to Faith*. The Guardian, 2nd June

HURCOMBE, T. (2001), *Disestablishing the Kingdom* in LEECH, K. (ED), *Setting the Church of England Free: The Case for Disestablishment*. Croydon: The Jubilee Group

Public Records Office. S.P. 1/70 pp 35-6

Stat. Realm, iii. 492

PODMORE, C. (2005), *Aspects of Anglican Identity*. Church House Publishing

PITT, V. (2001), *The Church by Law Established* in LEECH, K. (ED), *Setting the Church of England Free: The Case for Disestablishment*. Croydon: The Jubilee Group

SPONG, J. S. (2007), *Jesus for the Non-Religious*. New York: Harper Collins

WILLIAMS, R. (2007), *Tokens of Trust*. Norwich: Canterbury Press

JAMES, E. (1987), *A Life of Bishop John Robinson*. London: Collins

BUNCH, D. and RITCHIE, A. (EDs) (2009), *Prayer and Prophecy: The Essential Kenneth Leech*. London: Darton, Longman and Todd

BRUCE, S. (2007), *Paisley: Religion and Politics in Northern Ireland*. Oxford

FRASER, G. (2009), *Beware of the Dark Side of Liberalism*. The Church Times, 8th May

MacCULLOCH, D. (2009), *A History of Christianity*. London: Allen Lane

YATES, N. (2010), *Love Now Pay Later?* London: SPCK

THATCHER, A. (2011), *Reading the Bible Today*. Opening Address at the Modern Church Conference, July

NEWLANDS, G. M. (2012), *Humane Spirit: Towards a Liberal Theology of Resistance and Respect* in SUGIRTHARAJAH, S. (ED), *Religious Pluralism and the Modern World: An Ongoing Engagement with John Hick*. Basingstoke: Palgrave Macmillan

HOLLOWAY, R. (2012), *Leaving Alexandria: A Memoir of Faith and Doubt*. Edinburgh: Canongate Books

SAXBEE, J. (1994), *Liberal Evangelism: A Flexible Response to the Decade.* London: SPCK

SCILLEBEECKX, E. (1981), *Ministry: A Case for Change.* London: SCM Press

DAVISON, A. and MILBANK, A. (2010), *For the Parish: A Critique of Fresh Expressions.* London: SCM Press

MASON, K. (1992), *Priesthood and Society.* Norwich: Canterbury Press

HARDY, D. W. (2001), *Finding the Church.* London: SCM Press

RAMSEY, M. (1972), *The Christian Priest Today.* London: SPCK

KOTLER, P. (2003), *Marketing Insights from A to Z.* New Jersey: Wiley and Sons

MERCER, D. (1992), *Marketing.* Oxford: Blackwell

STEVENS, R. E. and LOUDON, D. L. (1992), *Marketing for Churches and Ministers.* New York: Haworth Press

HOLLOWAY, R. (1996), *Introduction* in JOHN, J. (ED), *Living Evangelism.* London: Darton, Longman and Todd

PERCY, M. (2006), *Many Rooms in my Father's House: The Changing Identity of the English Parish Church* in CROFT, S. (ED) *The Future of the Parish System.* London: Church House Publishing

QUASH, B. (2003), *The Anglican Church as a Polity of Presence* in DORMOR, D., McDONALD, J., and CADDICK, J. *Anglicanism: The Answer to Modernity.* London: Continuum

Circle Books

Circle is a symbol of infinity and unity. It's part of a growing list of imprints, including o-books.net and zero-books.net.

Circle Books aims to publish books in Christian spirituality that are fresh, accessible, and stimulating.

Our books are available in all good English language bookstores worldwide. If you can't find the book on the shelves, then ask your bookstore to order it for you, quoting the ISBN and title. Or, you can order online—all major online retail sites carry our titles.

To see our list of titles, please view www.Circle-Books.com, growing by 80 titles per year.

Authors can learn more about our proposal process by going to our website and clicking on Your Company > Submissions.

We define Christian spirituality as the relationship between the self and its sense of the transcendent or sacred, which issues in literary and artistic expression, community, social activism, and practices. A wide range of disciplines within the field of religious studies can be called upon, including history, narrative studies, philosophy, theology, sociology, and psychology. Interfaith in approach, Circle Books fosters creative dialogue with non-Christian traditions.

And tune into MySpiritRadio.com for our book review radio show, hosted by June-Elleni Laine, where you can listen to authors discussing their books.

MySpiritRadio